a defense of Calvinism

Great Christian Books
Lindenhurst, New York

C. H. Spurgeon

a defense of Calvinism

and select sermons on the doctrines of grace

A Spurgeon Classic

A GREAT CHRISTIAN BOOKS publication
Great Christian Books is an imprint of Rotolo Media
160 37th Street Lindenhurst, New York 11757 (631) 956-0998
www.GreatChristianBooks.com
email: mail@greatchristianbooks.com
A Defense of Calvinism ISBN 978-1-61010-130-1

Spurgeon, Charles Haddon, 1834-1892
A Defense of Calvinism / by Charles Haddon Spurgeon
p. cm.
A "A Great Christian Book" book
GREAT CHRISTIAN BOOKS a division of Rotolo Media
ISBN 978-1-61010-130-1
Recommended Dewey Decimal Classifications: 200, 230
Suggested Subject Headings:
1. Religion—Christian literature—Christianity & Christian theology
2. Christianity—The Bible—Soteriology
I. Title

The book and cover design for this title are by Michael Rotolo. It is typeset in the Minion and Myriad typefaces by Adobe Inc. and is quality manufactured in the United States on acid-free paper stock. To discuss the publication of your Christian manuscript or out-of-print book, please contact Great Christian Books.

MANUFACTURED IN THE UNITED STATES OF AMERICA

Contents

The old truth that Calvin preached, that Augustine preached, that Paul preached, is the truth that I must preach to-day, or else be false to my conscience and my God. I cannot shape the truth; I know of no such thing as paring off the rough edges of a doctrine. John Knox's gospel is my gospel. That which thundered through Scotland must thunder through England again.

—C. H. Spurgeon

This message is from
C. H. Spurgeon's Autobiography, Volume One.

A Defense of Calvinism

It is a great thing to begin the Christian life by believing good solid Doctrine. Some people have received 20 different "gospels" in as many years. How many more they will accept before they get to their journey's end, it would be difficult to predict. I thank God that He early taught me the Gospel, and I have been so perfectly satisfied with it, that I do not want to know any other. Constant change of creed is sure loss; if a tree has to be taken up two or three times a year, you will not need to build a very large loft in which to store the apples! When people are always shifting their doctrinal principles, they are not likely to bring forth much fruit to the Glory of God. It is good for young Believers to begin with a firm hold upon those great fundamental Doctrines which the Lord has taught in His Word; why if I believed what some preach about the temporary, trumpery salvation which only lasts for a time, I would scarcely be at all grateful for it; but when I know that those whom God saves, He saves with an everlasting salvation; when I know that He gives to them an everlasting righteousness; when I know that He settles them on an everlasting foundation of everlasting love, and that He will bring them to His everlasting Kingdom—oh, then I do wonder, and I am astonished that such a blessing as this should ever have been given to me!—

"Pause, my Soul! Adore and wonder!
Ask, 'Oh, why such love to me?'
Grace has put me in the number
Of the Savior's family:
Hallelujah!
Thanks, eternal thanks, to Thee."

I suppose there are some persons whose minds naturally incline towards the doctrine of free will; I can only say that mine inclines as naturally towards the Doctrines of Sovereign Grace! Sometimes, when I see some of the worst characters in the street, I feel as if my heart must burst forth in tears of gratitude that God has never let me act as they have done! I have thought if God had left me alone, and had not touched me by His Grace what a great sinner I would have been! I would have run to the utmost lengths of sin, and dived into the very depths of evil! Nor would I have stopped at any vice or folly, if God had not restrained me; I feel that I would have been a very king of sinners if God had let me alone. I cannot understand the reason why I am saved except upon the ground that God would have it so. I cannot, if I look ever so earnestly, discover any kind of reason in myself why I should be a partaker of Divine Grace. If I am at this moment with Christ, it is only because Christ Jesus would have His will with me, and that will was that I should be with Him where He is, and should share His

Glory. I can put the crown nowhere but upon the head of Him whose mighty Grace has saved me from going down into the pit of Hell!

Looking back on my past life, I can see that the dawning of it all was of God—of God effectively. I took no torch with which to light the sun, but the sun enlightened me. I did not commence my spiritual life—no, I rather kicked and struggled against the things of the Spirit. When He drew me, for a time I did not run after Him—there was a natural hatred in my soul of everything holy and good! Wooings were lost upon me—warnings were cast to the wind—thunders were despised. As for the whispers of His love, they were rejected as being less than nothing and vanity. But, sure I am, I can say now, speaking on behalf of myself, "He only is my salvation." It was He who turned my heart, and brought me down on my knees before Him. I can in very deed, say with Doddridge and Toplady—

"Grace taught my soul to pray,
And made my eyes overflow."

And coming to this moment, I can add—

"Tis Grace has kept me to this day,
And will not let me go."

Well can I remember the manner in which I learned the Doctrines of Grace in a single instant. Born, as all of us are by nature, an Arminian, I still believed the old things I had heard continually from the pulpit, and did not see the Grace of God. When I was coming to Christ, I thought I was doing it all myself, and though I sought the Lord earnestly, I had no idea the Lord was seeking me. I do not think the young convert is at first aware of this. I can recall the very day and hour when first I received those Truths in my own soul—when they were, as John Bunyan says, burnt into my heart as with a hot iron, and I can recollect how I felt that I had grown all of a sudden from a babe into a man—that I had made progress in Scriptural knowledge through having found, once and for all, the clue to the Truth of God. One week night, when I was sitting in the House of God, I was not thinking much about the preacher's sermon, for I did not believe it. The thought struck me, How did you come to be a Christian? I sought the Lord. But how did you come to seek the Lord? The truth flashed across my mind in a moment—I would not have sought Him unless there had been some previous influence in my mind to make me seek Him! I prayed, thought I, but then I asked myself, How came I to pray? I was induced to pray by reading the Scriptures. How came I to read the Scriptures? I did read them, but what led me to do so? Then, in a moment, I saw that God was at the bottom of it all, and that He was the Author of my faith—and so the whole Doctrine of Grace opened up to me and from that Doctrine I have not departed to this day, and I desire to make this my constant confession, "I ascribe my change wholly to God."

I once attended a service where the text happened to be, "He shall choose our inheritance for us"—and the good man who occupied the pulpit was more than a little of an Arminian. Therefore, when he commenced, he said, "This passage refers entirely to our temporal inheritance; it has nothing whatever to do with our everlasting destiny, for," he said, "we do not want Christ to choose for us in the matter of Heaven or Hell. It is so plain and easy that every man who has a grain of common sense will choose Heaven, and any person would know better than to choose Hell! We have no need of any superior intelligence, or any greater Being to choose Heaven or Hell for us; it is left to our own free will, and we have enough wisdom given us, sufficiently correct means to judge for ourselves." And therefore, as he very logically inferred, there was no necessity for Jesus Christ, or anyone, to make a choice for us; who could choose the inheritance for ourselves without any assistance. "Ah," I thought, "but, my good Brother, it may be very true that we could, but I think we would want something more than common sense before we would choose aright." First, let me ask, must we not all of us admit an overruling Providence and the appointment of Jehovah's hand as to the means whereby we came into this world? Those men who think that, afterwards, we are left to our own free will to choose this one, or the other to direct our steps, must admit that our entrance into the world was not of our own will, but that God had then to choose for us. What circumstances were those in our power which led us to elect certain persons to be our parents? Had we anything to do with it? Did not God Himself appoint our parents, native place and friends?

Could He not have caused me to be born with the skin of the Hottentot; brought forth by a filthy mother who would nurse me in her "kraal," and teach me to bow down to Pagan gods, quite as easily as to have given me a pious mother, who would each morning and night bend her knees in prayer on my behalf? Or, might He not, if He had pleased, have given me some profligate to have been my parent—from whose lips I might have early heard fearful, filthy, and obscene language? Might He not have placed me where I would have had a drunken father who would have immured me in a very dungeon of ignorance, and brought me up in the chains of crime? Was it not God's Providence that I had so happy a lot that both my parents were His children, and endeavored to train me up in the fear of the Lord? John Newton used to tell a whimsical story and laugh at it, too, of a good woman who said, in order to prove the Doctrine of Election, "Ah, Sir, the Lord must have loved me before I was born, or else He would not have seen anything in me to love afterwards." I am sure it is true in my case. I believe the Doctrine of Election because I am quite certain that if God had not chosen me, I would never have chosen Him; and I am sure He chose me before I was born, or else He never would have chosen me afterwards! He must have elected me for reasons unknown to me, for I never could find any reason in myself why He should have looked upon me with special love. So I am forced to accept that great Biblical Doctrine.

I recollect an Arminian Brother telling me that he had read the Scriptures through a score or more times and could never find the Doctrine of Election in them; he added that he was sure he would have done so if it had been there, for he read the Word on his knees. I said to him, "I think you read the Bible in a very uncomfortable posture, and if you had read it in your easy chair, you would have been more likely to understand it. Pray, by all means, and the more the better, but it is a piece of superstition to think there is anything in the posture in which a man puts himself for reading! As to reading through the Bible 20 times without having found anything about the Doctrine of Election, the wonder is that you found anything at all—you must have galloped through it at such a rate that you were not likely to have any intelligible idea of the meaning of the Scriptures." If it would be marvelous to see one river leap up from the earth, full-grown, what would it be to gaze upon a vast spring from which all the rivers of the earth should at once come bubbling up, a million of them born at a birth? What a vision would it be! Who can conceive it? And yet the love of God is that fountain, from which all the rivers of mercy which have ever gladdened our race—all the rivers of Grace in time and of glory hereafter—take their rise. My Soul, stand at that sacred fountainhead, and adore and magnify, forever and ever, God, even our Father, who has loved us! In the very beginning, when this great universe lay in the mind of God like unborn forests in the acorn cup—long before the echoes awoke the solitudes—before the mountains were brought forth; long before the light flashed through the sky, God loved His chosen creatures! Before there was any created being—when the ether was not fanned by an angel's wings; when space itself had not an existence; when there was nothing save God alone—even then, in that loneliness of Deity, and in that deep quiet and profundity, His heart moved with love for His chosen! Their names were written on His heart, and then were they dear to His soul! Jesus loved His people before the foundation of the world—even from eternity! And when He called me by His Grace, He said to me, "I have loved you with an everlasting love: therefore with loving kindness have I drawn you." Then, in the fullness of time, He purchased me with His blood; He let His heart run out in one deep gaping wound for me long before I loved Him! Yes, when He first came to me, did I not spurn Him? When He knocked at the door, and asked for entrance, did I not drive Him away and do despite to His Grace? Ah, I can remember that I full often did so until, at last, by the power of His effectual Grace, He said, "I must, I will come in." And then He turned my heart, and made me love Him—but even till now I would have resisted Him, had it not been for His Grace.

Well, since He purchased me when I was dead in sins, does it not follow, as a necessary and logical consequence, that He must have loved me first? Did my Savior die for me because I believed on Him? No. I was not then in existence! I had then no being. Could the Savior, therefore, have died because I had faith, when I was not yet born? Could that have been possible? Could that have been the origin of the Savior's love towards me? Oh, no! My Savior died for me long before I believed. "But," says someone, "He foresaw that you would have faith, and therefore He loved you." What did He foresee about my faith? Did He foresee that I should get that faith, myself, and that I should believe on Him of myself? No! Christ could not foresee that, because no Christian will ever say that faith came of itself without the gift, and without the working of the Holy Spirit. I have met with a great many Believers, and talked with them about this matter, but I never knew one who could put his hand on his heart and say, "I believed in Jesus without the assistance of the Holy Spirit." I am bound to the Doctrine of the Depravity of the Human Heart because I find myself depraved in heart, and have daily proofs that in my flesh there dwells no good thing! If God enters into Covenant with unfallen man, man is so insignificant a creature, that it must be an act of gracious condescension on the Lord's part; but if God enters into Covenant with sinful man, he is then so offensive a creature, that it must be, on God's part, an act of pure, free, rich, Sovereign Grace! When the Lord entered into Covenant with me, I am sure that it was all of Grace, nothing else but Grace; when I remember what a den of unclean beasts and birds my heart was, and how strong was my unrenewed will, how obstinate and rebellious against the sovereignty of the Divine rule, I always feel inclined to take the very lowest room in my Father's house; and when I enter Heaven, it will be to go among the less than the least of all saints, and with the chief of sinners.

The late lamented Mr. Denham has put, at the foot of his portrait, a most admirable text, "Salvation is of the Lord." That is just an epitome of Calvinism—it is the sum and substance of it—if anyone should ask me what I mean by a Calvinist, I would reply, "He is one who says Salvation is of the Lord." I cannot find in Scripture any other Doctrine than this; it is the essence of the Bible, "He only is my rock and my salvation." Tell me anything contrary to this Truth of God, and it will be a heresy! Tell me a heresy, and I shall find its essence here, that it has departed from this great, this fundamental, this rock Truth, "God is my rock and my salvation." What is the heresy of Rome, but the addition of something to the perfect merits of Jesus Christ—the bringing in of the works of the flesh to assist in our justification? And what is the heresy of Arminianism, but the addition of something to the work of the Redeemer? Every heresy, if brought to the touchstone, will discover itself here! I have my own private opinion that there is no such thing as preaching Christ, and Him crucified unless we preach what nowadays is called Calvinism; it is a nickname to call it Calvinism—Calvinism is the Gospel and nothing else! I do not believe we can preach the Gospel if we do not preach justification by faith, without works—nor unless we preach the Sovereignty of God in His dispensation of Grace—nor unless we exalt the electing, unchangeable, eternal, immutable, conquering love of Jehovah! Nor do I think we can preach the Gospel unless we base it upon the special and Particular Redemption of His elect and chosen people which Christ worked out upon the Cross. Nor can I comprehend a Gospel which lets saints fall away after they are called, and allows the children of God to be burned in the fires of damnation after having once believed in Jesus! Such a Gospel I abhor—

> **"If ever it should come to pass,**
> **That sheep of Christ might fall away,**
> **My fickle, feeble soul, alas!**
> **Would fall a thousand times a day."**

If one dear saint of God had perished, so might all! If one of the covenant ones is lost, so may all be! And then there is no Gospel promise true, but the Bible is a lie, and there is nothing in it worth my acceptance. I will be an infidel at once when I can believe that a saint of God can ever fall finally! If God has loved me once, then He will love me forever; God has a master-mind—He arranged everything in His gigantic intellect long before He did it—and once having settled it, He never alters it! "This shall be done," He says, and the iron hand of destiny marks it down, and it is brought to pass. "This is My purpose," and it stands—neither earth or Hell alter it. "This is My decree," He says, "promulgate it, you holy angels. Rend it down from the gate of Heaven, you devils, if you can—but you cannot alter the decree—it shall stand forever." God alters not His plans. Why should He? He is Almighty, and therefore can perform His pleasure. Why should He? He is the All-wise, and therefore cannot have planned wrongly. Why should He? He is the everlasting God, and therefore cannot die before His plan is accomplished. Why should He change? You worthless atoms of earth, ephemera of a day! You creeping insects upon this bay-leaf of existence—you may change your plans—but He shall never, never change His! Has He told me that His plan is to save me? If so, I am forever safe—

> **"My name from the palms of His hands**
> **Eternity will not erase**
> **Impressed on His heart it remains,**
> **In marks of indelible Grace."**

I do not know how some people who believe that a Christian can fall from Grace manage to be happy. It must be a very commendable thing in them to be able to get through a day without despair! If I did not believe the Doctrine of the Final Perseverance of the Saints, I think I would be, of all men, the most miserable, because I should lack any ground of comfort. I could not say, whatever state of heart I came into, that I should be like a well-spring of water whose stream fails not; I should rather have to take the comparison of an intermittent spring that might stop all of a sudden, or a reservoir which I had no reason to expect would always be full. I believe that the happiest of Christians, and the truest of Christians are those who never dare to doubt God, but who take His Word simply as it stands, and believe it and ask no questions—just feeling assured that if God has said it, it will be so. I bear my willing testimony that I have no reason, nor even the shadow of a reason, to doubt my Lord, and I challenge Heaven and earth, and Hell to bring any proof that God is untrue! From the depths of Hell I call the fiends, and from this earth I call the tried and afflicted Believers, and to Heaven I appeal and challenge the long experience of the blood-washed host—and there is not to be found in the three realms, a single person who can bear witness to one fact which can disprove the faithfulness of God, or weaken His claim to be trusted by His servants! There are many things that may or may not happen, but this I know shall happen—

"He shall present my soul,
Unblemished and complete,
Before the glory of His face,
With joys divinely great."

All the purposes of man have been defeated, but not the purposes of God! The promises of man may be broken—many of them are made to be broken—but the promises of God shall all be fulfilled! He is a promise-maker, but He never was a promise-breaker; He is a promise-keeping God, and every one of His people shall prove it to be so. This is my grateful, personal confidence, "The Lord will perfect that which concerns me"—unworthy me, lost and ruined me! He will yet save me. And—

"I, among the blood-washed throng,
Shall wave the palm and wear the crown,
And shout loud victor."

I go to a land which the plow of earth has never upturned; where it is greener than earth's best pastures. and richer than her most abundant harvests ever saw! I go to a building of more gorgeous architecture than man has ever built—it is not of mortal design—it is "a building of God, a house not made with hands, eternal in the Heavens." All I shall know and enjoy in Heaven will be given to me by the Lord, and I shall say, when at last I appear before Him—

"Grace all the work shall crown
Through everlasting days;
It lays in Heaven the topmost stone,
And well deserves the praise."

I know there are some who think it necessary to their system of theology to limit the merit of the blood of Jesus—if my theological system needed such a limitation, I would cast it to the winds! I cannot, I dare not, allow the thought to find a lodging in my mind—it seems so near akin to blasphemy. In Christ's finished work, I see an ocean of merit; my plummet finds no bottom, my eye discovers no shore. There is sufficient efficacy in the blood of Christ, if God had so willed it, to have saved not only all in this world, but all in ten thousand worlds had they transgressed their Maker's Law! Once admit infinity into the matter, and limit is out of the question! Having a Divine Person for an Offering, it is not consistent to conceive of limited value; boundaries and measure are inapplicable terms to the Divine Sacrifice! The intent of the Divine Purpose fixes the application of the Infinite Offering, but does not change it into a finite work. Think of the numbers upon whom God has bestowed His Grace; think of the countless hosts in Heaven—if you were introduced there today, you would find it as easy to count the stars, or the sands of the sea, as to count the multitudes that are before the Throne even now! They have come from the East and from the West, from the North and from the South, and they are sitting down with Abraham and with Isaac, and with Jacob in the Kingdom of God.

Beside those in Heaven, think of the saved ones on earth. Blessed be God, His Elect on earth are to be counted by millions! I believe the days are coming, brighter days than these, when there shall be multitudes upon multitudes brought to know the Savior, and to rejoice in Him. The Father's love is not only for a few, but for an exceedingly great company. "A great multitude, which no man could number," will be found in Heaven! A man can reckon up to very high figures; set to work your Newtons, your mightiest calculators, and they can count great numbers; but God, and God alone, can tell the multitude of His redeemed! I believe there will be more in Heaven than in Hell. If anyone asks me why I think so, I answer, because Christ, in everything, is to "have the pre-eminence," and I cannot conceive how He could have the pre-eminence if there are to be more in the dominions of Satan than in Paradise. Moreover, I have never read that there is to be in Hell a great multitude which no man could number. I rejoice to know that the souls of all infants, as soon as they die, speed their way to Paradise; think what a multitude there is of them! Then there are already in Heaven unnumbered myriads of the spirits of just men made perfect—the redeemed of all nations and kindreds and people, and tongues up till now. And there are better times coming, when the religion of Christ shall be universal—

> **"He shall reign from pole to pole,**
> **With illimitable sway,"**

when whole kingdoms shall bow down before Him, and nations shall be born in a day, and in the thousand years of the great millennial state, there will be enough saved to make up all the deficiencies of the thousands of years that have gone before! Christ shall be Master everywhere, and His praise shall be sounded in every land. Christ shall have the pre-eminence at last; His train shall be far larger than that which shall attend the chariot of the grim monarch of Hell!

Some persons love the doctrine of universal atonement, because, they say, "It is so beautiful. It is a lovely idea that Christ should have died for all men. It commends itself," they say, "to the instincts of humanity! There is something in it full of joy and beauty." I admit there is, but beauty may be often associated with lies! There is much which I might admire in the theory of universal redemption, but I will just show what the supposition necessarily involves. If Christ on His Cross intended to save every man, then He intended to save those who were lost before He died; if the doctrine is true—that He died for all men—then He died for some who were in Hell before He came into this world—for doubtless there were even then myriads there who had been cast away because of their sins! Once again—if it were Christ's intention to save all men, how deplorably has He been disappointed, for we have His own testimony that there is a lake which burns with fire and brimstone, and into that pit of woe have been cast some of the very persons who, according to the theory of universal redemption, were bought with His blood! That seems to me a conception a thousand times more repulsive than any of those consequences which are said to be associated with the Calvinistic and Christian Doctrine of special and Particular Redemption! To think that my Savior died for men who were, or are in Hell, seems a supposition too horrible for me to entertain! To imagine for a moment that He was the Substitute for all the sons of men, and that God, having first punished the Substitute, afterwards punished the sinners, seems to conflict with all my ideas of Divine Justice; that Christ should offer an atonement and satisfaction for the sins of all men, and that afterwards some of those very men should be punished for the sins for which Christ had already atoned, appears to me to be the most monstrous iniquity that could ever have been imputed to Saturn, to Janus, to the goddess of the Thugs, or to the most diabolical heathen deities! God forbid that we should ever think thus of Jehovah, the Just and Wise and Good!

There is no soul living who holds more firmly to the Doctrines of Grace than I do, and if any man asks me whether I am ashamed to be called a Calvinist, I answer—I wish to be called nothing but a Christian—but if you ask me, do I hold the doctrinal views which were held by John Calvin? I reply I do in the main hold them, and rejoice to avow it; but far be it from me even to imagine that Zion contains none but Calvinistic Christians within her walls, or that there are none saved who do not hold our views! Most atrocious things have been spoken about the character and spiritual condition of John Wesley, the modem prince of Arminians. I can only say concerning him, that while I detest many of the doctrines which he preached, yet for the man, himself, I have a reverence second to no Wesleyan. And if there were needed two Apostles to be added to the number of the twelve, I do not believe that there could be found two men more fit to be so added than George Whitefield, and John Wesley! The character of John Wesley stands beyond all imputation for self-sacrifice, zeal, holiness, and communion with God. He lived far above the ordinary level of common Christians, and was one "of whom the world was not worthy." I believe there are multitudes of men who cannot see these truths of Calvinism, or, at least, cannot see them in the way in which we put them, who nevertheless have received Christ as their Savior, and are as dear to the heart of the

God of Grace as the most sound Calvinist in or out of Heaven. I do not think I differ from any of my Hyper-Calvinistic Brothers and Sisters in what I do believe, but I differ from them in what they do not believe. I do not hold any less than they do, but I hold a little more, and I think, a little more of the Truth of God revealed in the Scriptures. Not only are there a few cardinal Doctrines by which we can steer our ship North, South, East, or West, but as we study the Word, we shall begin to learn something about the Northwest, and Northeast, and all else that lies between the four cardinal points. The system of Truth revealed in the Scriptures is not simply one straight line, but two—no man will ever get a right view of the Gospel until he knows how to look at the two lines at once. For instance, I read in one Book of the Bible, "The Spirit and the bride say, Come. And let him that hears say, Come. And let him that is thirsty come; and whoever wills, let him take the water of life freely." Yet I am taught, in another part of the same Inspired Word, that, "it is not of him who wills, nor of him who runs, but of God who shows mercy." I see in one place God in Providence presiding over all, and yet I see, and I cannot help seeing that man acts as he pleases, and that God has left his actions, in a great measure, to his own free will.

Now, if I were to declare that man was so free to act that there was no control of God over his actions, I would be driven very near to atheism. But if, on the other hand, I should declare that God so overrules all things that man is not free enough to be responsible, I would be driven at once into Antinomianism or fatalism. That God predestines, and yet that man is responsible, are two facts that few can clearly see; they are believed to be inconsistent, and contradictory to each other. If, then, I find taught in one part of the Bible that everything is foreordained—that is true; and if I find, in another Scripture, that man is responsible for all his actions—that is true! It is only my folly that leads me to imagine that these two Truths of God can ever contradict each other! I do not believe they can ever be welded into one upon any earthly anvil—but they certainly shall be one in eternity. They are two lines that are so nearly parallel, that the human mind which pursues them farthest will never discover that they converge—but they do converge—and they will meet somewhere in eternity, close to the Throne of God, where all of His Truths spring!

It is often said that the Doctrines we believe, have a tendency to lead us to sin; I have heard it asserted most positively that those high Doctrines which we love, and which we find in the Scriptures, are licentious ones! I do not know who will have the hardihood to make that assertion when they consider that the holiest of men have been believers in them. I ask the man who dares to say that Calvinism is a licentious religion, what he thinks of the character of Augustine, or Calvin, or Whitefield, who in successive ages were the great exponents of the system of Grace? Or what will he say of the Puritans, whose works are full of them? Had a man been an Arminian in those days, he would have been accounted the vilest heretic breathing; but now we are looked upon as the heretics, and they as the orthodox! We have gone back to the old school; we can trace our descent from the Apostles; it is that vein of free Grace running through the sermonizing of Baptists which has saved us as a denomination! Were it not for that, we should not stand where we are today. We can run a golden line up to Jesus Christ, Himself, through a holy succession of mighty fathers who all held these glorious Truths—and we can ask concerning them—"Where will you find holier and better men in the world?" No Doctrine is so calculated to preserve a man from sin as the Doctrine of the Grace of God—those who have called it "a licentious Doctrine"—did not know anything at all about it. Poor ignorant things—they little knew that their own vile stuff was the most licentious doctrine under Heaven; if they knew the Grace of God in truth, they would soon see that there was no preservative from lying like a knowledge that we are elect of God from the foundation of the world; there is nothing like a belief in my eternal perseverance, and the immutability of my Father's affection which can keep me near to Him from a motive of simple gratitude! Nothing makes a man so virtuous as belief of the Truths of God! A lying doctrine will soon beget a lying practice; a man cannot have an erroneous belief without, by-and-by, having an erroneous life. I believe the one thing naturally begets the other. Of all men—those have the most disinterested piety, the most sublime reverence, the most ardent devotion—who believe that they are saved by Grace, without works, through faith, and that not of themselves, it is the gift of God! Christians should take heed and see that it always is so, lest by any means Christ should be crucified afresh, and put to an open shame.

MISREPRESENTATIONS OF TRUE CALVINISM CLEARED AWAY

In 1861, the church of which Mr. C. H. Spurgeon was pastor, completed its tremendous new structure, the Metropolitan Tabernacle. The first sermon by Mr. Spurgeon in this new building was preached on Monday afternoon, March 25th. A few days later in this new building, on Thursday, April 1st, Mr. Spurgeon had what we would commonly call a Bible conference. The theme being, "Exposition of the Doctrines of Grace." The speakers and their subjects were as follows—

Election by John Bloomfield;
Human Depravity by Evan Probert;
Particular Redemption by James A. Spurgeon, Mr. Spurgeon's brother;
Effectual Calling by James Smith, and
The Final Perseverance of Believers in Christ Jesus by William O'Neil.

Mr. Spurgeon, served as the Master of Ceremonies, and gave the following introductory message to the conference. The main body of this message is as follows—

Excerpted from The New Park Street and Metropolitan Tabernacle Pulpit, Volume 7.

MISREPRESENTATIONS OF TRUE CALVINISM CLEARED AWAY

THERE IS NOTHING UPON which men need to be more instructed than upon the question of what Calvinism really is. The most infamous allegations have been brought against us, and sometimes, I must fear, by men who knew them to be utterly untrue; and to this day there are many of our opponents who, when they run short of matter, invent and make for themselves a man of straw! They call that man of straw, John Calvin, and then shoot all their arrows at it. We have not come here to defend your man of straw; shoot at him or burn him as you will, and if it suits your convenience, go ahead and still oppose doctrines which were never taught, and rail at fictions which, save in your brain, were never in existence! We come here to state what our views really are, and we trust that any who do not agree with us will do us the justice of not misrepresenting us. If they can disprove our Doctrines, let them state them fairly, and then overthrow them—but why should they first caricature our opinions, and then afterwards attempt to put them down?

Among the gross falsehoods which have been uttered against the Calvinists proper is the wicked calumny that we hold the damnation of little infants. A baser lie was never uttered! There may have existed somewhere—in some corner of the earth—a miscreant who would dare to say that there were infants in Hell, but I have never met with him, nor have I met with a man who ever saw such a person. We say, with regard to infants, Scripture said but very little, and therefore, where Scripture is confessedly scant, it is for no man to determine dogmatically; but I think I speak for the entire body, or certainly with exceedingly few exceptions, and those unknown to me, when I say we hold that all infants are elect of God, and are, therefore, saved, and we look to this as being the means by which Christ shall see of the travail of His soul to a great degree, and we do sometimes hope that thus the multitude of the saved shall be made to exceed the multitude of the lost. Whatever views our friends may hold upon the point, they are not necessarily connected with Calvinistic Doctrine. I believe that the Lord Jesus, who said, "Of such is the Kingdom of Heaven," does daily and constantly receive into His loving arms those tender ones who are only shown, and then snatched away to Heaven. Our hymns are no ill witness to our faith on this point, and one of them runs thus—

"Millions of infant souls compose
The family above."

Toplady, one of the keenest of Calvinists, was of this number. "In my remarks," he says, "on Dr. Newell, I testified my firm belief that the souls of all departed infants are with God in Glory—that in the decree of predestination to life, God has included all whom He decreed to take away in infancy—and that the decree of reprobation has nothing to do with them." No, he proceeds farther, and asks, with reason, how the anti-Calvinistic system of conditional salvation, and election, or good works foreseen, will suit with the salvation of infants? It is plain that Arminians and Pelagians must introduce a new principle of election—and in so far as the salvation of infants is concerned, become Calvinists! Is it not an argument in behalf of Calvinism that its principle is uniform throughout, and that no change is needed on the ground on which man is saved, whether young or old? John Newton, of London, the friend of Cowper, noted for his Calvinism, holds that the children in Heaven exceed its adult inhabitants in all their multitudinous array! Gill, a very champion of Calvinism, held the Doctrine that all dying in infancy are saved; an intelligent modem writer, Dr. Russell of Dundee, also a Calvinist, maintains the same views. When it is considered that nearly one-half of the human race die in early years, it is easy to see what a vast accession must be daily and hourly making to the blessed population of Heaven!

A more common charge, brought by more decent people, for I must say that the last charge is never brought except by disreputable persons—a more common charge is that we hold clear fatalism! Now, there may be Calvinists who are fatalists, but Calvinism and fatalism are two distinct things. Do not most Christians hold the Doctrine of the Providence of God?

Do not all Christians; do not all Believers in God hold the Doctrine of His foreknowledge? All the difficulties which are laid against the Doctrine of Predestination might, with equal force, be laid against that of Divine foreknowledge. We believe that God has predestinated all things from the beginning, but there is a difference between the predestination of an intelligent, All-Wise, All-Bounteous God, and that blind fatalism which simply says, "It is because it is to be." Between the predestination of Scripture, and the fate of the Koran, every sensible man must perceive a difference of the most essential character. We do not deny that the thing is so ordained that it must be, but why is it to be but that the Father—God—whose name is Love, ordained it? Not because of any necessity in circumstances that such-andsuch a thing should take place; though the wheels of Providence revolve with rigid exactness, yet not without purpose and wisdom! The wheels are full of eyes, and everything ordained is so ordained that it shall conduce to the grandest of all ends—the Glory of God—and next to that, the good of His creatures.

But we are next met by some who tell us that we preach the wicked and horrible doctrine of sovereign and unmerited reprobation. "Oh," they say, "you teach that men are damned because God made them to be damned, and that they go to Hell, not because of sin, not because of unbelief—but because of some dark decree with which God has stamped their destiny." Brothers and Sisters, this is an another unfair charge! Election does not involve reprobation! There may be some who hold unconditional reprobation, but I stand not here as their defender—let them defend themselves as best they can! I hold God's Election, but I testify just as clearly that if any man is lost, he is lost for sin. This has been the uniform statement of Calvinistic ministers. I might refer you to our standards such as "The Westminster Assembly's Catechism" and to all our Confessions, for they all distinctly state that man is lost for sin, and that there is no punishment put on any man except that which he richly and righteously deserves. If any of you have ever uttered that libel against us, do it not again—for we are as guiltless of that as you are yourselves! I am speaking personally—and I think in this I would command the suffrages of my Brothers—I do know that the appointment of God extends to all things; I stand not in this pulpit, nor in any other to lay the damnation of any man anywhere but upon himself! If he is lost, damnation is all of men. But, if he is saved, salvation is still all of God.

To state this important point yet more clearly and explicitly, I shall quote at large from an able Presbyterian divine—"The pious Methodist is taught that the Calvinist represents God as creating men in order to destroy them; he is taught that Calvinists hold that men are lost, not because they sin, but because they are non-elected. Believing this to be a true statement, is it not amazing that the Methodist stops short, and declares himself, if not an Arminian, at least an Anti-Predestinarian? But no statement can be more scandalously untrue. It is the uniform Doctrine of Calvinism that God creates all for His own Glory—that He is infinitely righteous and kind, and that where men perish, it is only for their sins. In speaking of suffering, whether in this world, or in the world to come—whether it respects angels or men, the Westminster standards (which may be considered as the most authoritative modern statement of the system) invariably connect the punishment with previous sin, and sin only—'As for those wicked and ungodly men whom God, as a righteous Judge, FOR their SINS does blind and harden, from them He not only withholds His Grace, whereby they might have been enlightened in their understandings, and worked upon in their hearts, but sometimes also withdraws the gifts which they had, and exposes them to such objects as their corruption makes occasion of sin; and withal gives them over to their own lusts, the temptations of the world and the power of Satan, whereby it comes to pass that they harden themselves even under those means which God uses for the softening of others.'

"The Larger Catechism, speaking of the unsaved among angels and men, says, 'God, according to His Sovereign power, and the unsearchable counsel of His own will (whereby He extends or withholds favor as He pleases) has passed by and foreordained the rest to dishonor and wrath, to before their sin inflicted, to the praise of the glory of His justice.' Again, 'the end of God appointing this day (of the last judgment) is for the manifestation of the glory of His mercy, in the eternal salvation of the elect, and of His justice in the damnation of the reprobate who are wicked and disobedient.'

"This is no more than what the Methodist and all other Evangelical bodies acknowledge—that where men perish it is in consequence of their sin. If it is asked why sin which destroys is permitted to enter the world, that is a question which bears not only on the Calvinist, but equally on all other parties. They are as much concerned and bound to answer it as he. No, the question is not confined to Christians. All who believe in the existence of God—in His righteous character and perfect Providence are equally under obligation to answer it. Whatever may be the reply of others, that of the Calvinist may be regarded as given in the statement of the Confession of Faith, which declares that God's Providence extends itself even to the first Fall and other sins of angels and men, etc.—Yet so as the sinfulness thereof proceeds only from the creature and not from God, who, being most holy and righteous, neither is nor can be 'the author or approver of sin.' It is difficult to see what more could be said upon the subject; and if such is the undoubted sentiments of Calvinists, then what misrepresentation can be more gross than that which describes them as holding that sinners perish irrespective of their sin, or that God is the Author of their sin? What is the declaration of Calvin? 'Every soul departs (at death) to that place which it has prepared for itself while in this world.' It is hard to be charged with holding as sacred Truth what one abhors as horrid blasphemy, and yet this is the treatment which has been perseveringly meted out to Calvinists in spite of the most solemn and indignant disclaimers! Against nothing have they more stoutly protested than the thought that the infinitely holy and righteous, and amiable Jehovah is the Author of sin—and yet how often do the supporters of rival systems charge them with this as an article of faith?"

A yet further charge against us is that we dare not preach the Gospel to the unregenerate! That, in fact, our theology is so narrow and cramped, that we cannot preach to sinners! Gentlemen, if you dare to say this, I would take you to any library in the world where the old Puritan fathers are stored up, and I would let you take down any one volume and tell me if you ever read more telling exhortations and addresses to sinners in any of your own books! Did not Bunyan plead with sinners and whoever classed him with any but the Calvinists? Did not Charnock, Goodwin, and Howe agonize for souls, and what were they but Calvinists? Did not Jonathan Edwards preach to sinners, and who more clear and explicit on these doctrinal matters? The works of our innumerable divines teem with passionate appeals to the unconverted! Oh, Sirs, if I should begin the list, time should fail me; it is an indisputable fact that we have labored more than they all for the winning of souls! Was George Whitefield any the less seraphic? Did his eyes weep the fewer tears or his heart move with less compassion because he believed in God's electing love, and preached the Sovereignty of the Most High? It is an unfounded calumny! Our souls are not stony; our hearts are not withdrawn from the compassion which we ought to feel for our fellow men; we can hold all our views, and yet can weep as Christ did over a Jerusalem which was certainly to be destroyed! Again I must say I am not defending certain Brothers who have exaggerated Calvinism. I speak of Calvinism proper—not that which has run to seed, and outgrown its beauty and verdure. I speak of it as I find it in Calvin's Institutes, and especially in his Expositions. I have read them carefully. I take not my views of Calvinism from common repute, but from his books; nor do I, in thus speaking, even vindicate Calvinism as if I cared for the name, but I mean that glorious system which teaches that salvation is of Grace from first to last! And again, then, I say it is an utterly unfounded charge that we dare not preach to sinners!

And then further, that I may clear up these points, and leave the less rubbish for my Brothers to wheel away—we have sometimes heard it said, but those who say it ought to go to school to read the first book of history—that we who hold Calvinistic views are the enemies of revivals. Why, Sirs, in the history of the Church, with but few exceptions, you could not find a revival at all that was not produced by the orthodox faith! What was that great work which was done by Augustine when the Church suddenly woke up from the pestiferous and deadly sleep into which Pelagian Doctrine had cast it? What was the Reformation, itself, but the waking up of men's minds to those old Truths of God? However far modern Lutherans may have turned aside from their ancient Doctrines—and I must confess some of them would not agree with what I now say, yet, at any rate—Luther and Calvin had no dispute about Predestination! Their views were identical, and Luther's, On the Bondage of the Will is as strong a book upon the Free Grace of God as Calvin, himself, could have written. Hear that great thunder while he cries in that book, "Let the Christian reader know, then, that God foresees nothing in a contingent manner—but that

He foresees, proposes, and acts from His eternal and unchangeable will! This is the thunder stroke which breaks and overturns free will." Need I mention to you better names than Huss, Jerome of Prague, Fartel, John Knox, Wickliffe, Wishart, and Bradford? Need I do more than say that these held the same views, and that in their day anything like an Arminian revival was utterly unheard of and undreamed of? And then, to come to more modem times, there is the great exception—that wondrous revival under Mr. Wesley in which the Wesleyan Methodists had so large a share. But permit me to say that the strength of the doctrine of Wesleyan Methodism lay in its Calvinism! The great body of the Methodists disclaimed Pelagianism in whole and in part; they contended for man's entire depravity, the necessity of the direct agency of the Holy Spirit, and that the first step in the change proceeds not from the sinner, but from God. They denied at the time that they were Pelagians; does not the Methodist hold as firmly as ever we do, that man is saved by the operation of the Holy Spirit and only the Holy Spirit?

And are not many of Mr. Wesley's sermons full of that great Truth—that the Holy Spirit is necessary to regeneration? Whatever mistakes he may have made, he continually preached the absolute necessity of the new birth by the Holy Spirit! And there are some other points of exceedingly close agreement; for instance, even that of human inability. It matters not how some may abuse us when we say man could not of himself repent or believe—yet the old Arminian standards said the same. True, they affirm that God has given Grace to every man, but they do not dispute the fact, that apart from that Grace, there was no ability in man to do that which was good in his own salvation. And then let me say—if you turn to the continent of America, how gross the falsehood that Calvinistic Doctrine is unfavorable to revivals! Look at that wondrous shaking under Jonathan Edwards and others which we might quote. Or turn to Scotland—what shall we say of M'Cheyne? What shall we say of those renowned Calvinists—Chalmers, Wardlaw, and before them, Livingstone, Haldane, Erskine, and the like? What shall we say of the men of their school but that, while they held and preached unflinchingly the great Truths which we would propound today, yet God acknowledged, their word and multitudes were saved? And if it were not perhaps too much like boasting of one's own work under God, I might say personally I have never found the preaching of these Doctrines lull this Church to sleep! But always while we have loved to maintain these Truths of God, we have agonized for the souls of men, and the 1,600 or more whom I have myself baptized, upon profession of their faith, are living testimonies that these old Truths in modern times have not lost their power to promote a revival of religion!

I have thus cleared away these allegations at the outset. I shall now need a few minutes more to say, with regard to the Calvinistic system, that there are some things to be said in its layout to which, of course, I attach but little comparative importance; but they ought not to be ignored. It is a fact that the system of Doctrines called the Calvinistic, is so exceedingly simple, and so readily learned, that as a system of Divinity it is more easily taught, and more easily grasped by unlettered minds than any other. The poor have the Gospel preached to them in a style which assists their memories, and commends itself to their judgments; it is a system which was practically acknowledged on high philosophic grounds by such men as Bacon, Leibnitz and Newton, and yet it can charm the soul of a child, and expand the intellect of a peasant! And then it has another virtue. I take it that the last is no mean one, but it has another—that when it is preached, there is a something in it which excites thought. A man may hear sermons upon the other theory which shall glance over him as the swallow's wing gently sweeps the brook—but these old Doctrines either make a man so angry, that he goes home, and cannot sleep for very hatred—or else they bring him down into lowliness of thought, feeling the immensity of the things which he has heard! Either way, it excites and stirs him up not temporarily, but in a most lasting manner. These Doctrines haunt him; he kicks against the pricks, and full often the Word forces a way into his soul! And I think this is no small thing for any Doctrine to do—in an age given to slumber, and with human hearts so indifferent to the Truth of God. I know that many men have gained more good by being made angry under a sermon than by being pleased by it—for being angry, they have turned the Truth of God over and over again, and at last that Truth has burned its way right into their hearts!

It also has this singular virtue—it is so coherent in all its parts. You cannot vanquish a Calvinist; you may think you can, but you cannot! The stones of the great

Doctrines so fit into each other that the more pressure there is applied to remove them, the more strenuously do they adhere. And you may mark that you cannot receive one of these Doctrines without believing all! Hold, for instance, that man is utterly depraved, and you draw the inference, then, that certainly if God has such a creature to deal with, salvation must come from God alone! And if from Him, the Offended One, to an offending creature—then He has a right to give or withhold His mercy as He wills—you are thus forced upon Election, and when you have gotten that, you have all—the others must follow. Some, by putting the strain upon their judgments, may manage to hold two or three points, and not the rest; but sound logic, I take it, requires a man to hold the whole or reject the whole! The Doctrines stand like soldiers in a square, presenting on every side a line of defense which is hazardous to attack, but easy to maintain. And mark you—in these times when error is so rife, and neology strives to be so rampant, it is no little thing to put into the hands of a young man a weapon which can slay his foes—a weapon he can easily learn to handle—which he may grasp tenaciously, wield readily, and carry without fatigue. A weapon, I may add, which no rust can corrode, and no blows can break—effective and well annealed—a true Jerusalem blade of a temper fit for deeds of renown! The coherency of the parts, though it is, of course, but a trifle in comparison with other things, is not unimportant.

And then, I add, but this is the point my Brothers will take up—it has this excellency—that it is Scriptural, and that it is consistent with the experience of Believers. Men generally grow more Calvinistic as they advance in years. Is not that a sign that the Doctrine is right? As they are growing riper for Heaven; as they are getting nearer to the rest that remains for the people of God; the soul longs to feed on the finest of the wheat and abhors chaff and husks. And then, I add—and, in so doing, I would refute a calumny that has sometimes been urged—this glorious Truth has this excellency, that it produces the holiest of men. We can look back through all our annals and say, to those who oppose us, you can mention no names of men more holy, more devoted, more loving, more generous than those which we can mention! The saints of our calendar, though economized by Rome, rank first in the Book of Life; the name of Puritan needs only to be heard to compel our reverence; holiness has reached a height among them which is rare, indeed, and well it might, for they loved and lived the Truth of God! And if you say that our Doctrine is harmful to human liberty, we point you to Oliver Cromwell, and to his brave Ironsides, Calvinists to a man! If you say it leads to inaction, we point you to the Pilgrim Fathers, and the wilderness they subdued. We can put our finger upon every spot of land the wide world over, and say, "Here was something done by a man who believed in God's Decrees, and, inasmuch as he did this, it is proof it did not make him inactive, it did not lull him to sloth."

The better way, however, of proving this point, is for each of us who hold these Truths of God to be more prayerful, more watchful, more holy, more active than we have ever been before, and by so doing, we shall put to silence the gainsaying of foolish men! A living argument is an argument which tells upon every man. We cannot deny what we see and feel. Be it ours, if maligned, to disprove it by a blameless life, and it shall yet come to pass that our Church and its sentiments, too, shall come forth,—

> **"Fair as the moon,**
> **clear as the sun,**
> **and terrible as an army with banners."**

Pray the Holy Spirit will use this message to bring many to a saving knowledge of Jesus Christ.

Sermon No. 182
Delivered March 7th, 1858
by Rev. C. H. Spurgeon
at The Music Hall, Royal Surrey Gardens

Total Depravity (Human Inability)

"No man can come to Me, except the Father who sent Me draws him."

— John 6:44

"COMING to Christ" is a very common phrase in Holy Scripture. It is used to express those acts of the soul wherein leaving at once our self-righteousness and our sins, we fly unto the Lord Jesus Christ and receive His righteousness to be our covering and His blood to be our atonement. Coming to Christ, then, embraces in it repentance, self-negation and faith in the Lord Jesus Christ. It sums within itself all those things which are the necessary attendants of these great states of heart, such as the belief of the Truths of God, earnestness of prayer to God, the submission of the soul to the precepts of God's Gospel and all those things which accompany the dawn of salvation in the soul. Coming to Christ is just the one essential thing for a sinner's salvation. He that comes not to Christ, do what he may, or think what he may, is yet in "the gall of bitterness and in the bonds of iniquity." Coming to Christ is the very first effect of regeneration. No sooner is the soul quickened than it at once discovers its lost estate, is horrified thereat, looks out for a refuge and believing Christ to be a suitable one, flies to Him and reposes in Him. Where there is not this coming to Christ, it is certain that there is as yet no quickening—where there is no quickening, the soul is dead in trespasses and sins—and being dead it cannot enter into the Kingdom of Heaven. We have before us now a very startling announcement—some say very obnoxious. Coming to Christ, though described by some people as being the very easiest thing in all the world, is in our text declared to be a thing utterly and entirely impossible to any man unless the Father shall draw him to Christ. It shall be our business, then, to enlarge upon this declaration. We doubt not that it will always be offensive to carnal nature, but nevertheless, the offending of human nature is sometimes the first step towards bringing it to bow itself before God. And if this is the effect of a painful process, we can forget the pain and rejoice in the glorious consequences!

I shall endeavor this morning, first of all, to notice man's inability, wherein it consists. Secondly, the Father's drawings—what these are and how they are exerted upon the soul. And then I shall conclude by noticing a sweet consolation which may be derived from this seemingly barren and terrible text.

I. First, then, MAN'S INABILITY. The text says, "No man can come to Me, except the Father who sent Me draws him." Wherein does this inability lie?

First, it does not lie in any physical defect. If in coming to Christ, moving the body or walking with the feet should be of any assistance, certainly man has all physical power to come to Christ in that sense. I remember to have heard a very foolish Antinomian declare that he did not believe any man had the power to walk to the House of God unless the Father drew him. Now the man was plainly foolish because he must have seen that as long as a man was alive and had legs, it was as easy for him to walk to the House of God as to the house of Satan! If coming to Christ includes the utterance of a prayer, man has no physical defect in that respect. If he is not dumb, he can say a prayer as easily as he can utter blasphemy. It is as easy for a man to sing one of the songs of Zion as to sing a profane and libidinous song. There is no lack of physical power in coming to Christ that can be needed with regard to the bodily strength man most assuredly has. And any part of salvation which consists in that is totally and entirely in the power of man without any assistance from the Spirit of God. Nor, again, does this inability lie in any mental lack. I can believe this Bible to be true just as easily as I can believe any other book to be true. So far as believing on Christ is an act of the mind, I am just as able to believe on Christ as I am able to believe on anybody else. Let his statement be but true, it is idle to tell me I cannot believe it. I can believe the statement that Christ makes as well as I can believe the statement of any other person. There is no deficiency of faculty in the mind—it is as capable of appreciating as a mere mental act the guilt of sin as it is of appreciating the guilt of assassination! It is just as possible for me to exercise the mental idea of seeking God as it is to exercise the thought of ambition. I have all the mental strength and power that can possibly be needed, so far as mental power is needed in salvation at all. No, there is not any man so ignorant that he can plead a lack of intellect as an excuse for rejecting the Gospel. The defect, then, does not lie either in the body, or what we are bound to call, speaking theologically, the mind. It is not any lack or deficiency there, although it is the vitiation of the mind—the corruption or the ruin of it—which, after all, is the very essence of man's inability!

Permit me to show you wherein this inability of man really does lie. It lies deep in his nature. Through the Fall and through our own sin, the nature of man has become so debased, depraved and corrupt, that it is impossible for him to come to Christ without the assistance of God the Holy Spirit! Now, in trying to exhibit how the nature of man thus renders him unable to come to Christ, you must allow me just to take this figure. You see a sheep—how willingly it feeds upon the herbage! You never knew a sheep to seek after carrion, it could not live on lion's food. Now bring me a wolf and you ask me whether a wolf cannot eat grass, whether it cannot be just as docile and as domesticated as the sheep. I answer, no, because its nature is contrary to it. You say, "Well, it has ears and legs. Can it not hear the shepherd's voice and follow him wherever he leads it?" I answer, certainly. There is no physical cause why it cannot do so, but its nature forbids it—and therefore I say it cannot do so. Can it not be tamed? Cannot its ferocity be removed? Probably it may so far be subdued that it may become apparently tame, but there will always be a marked distinction between it and the sheep, because there is a distinction in nature. Now, the reason why man cannot come to Christ is not because he cannot come, so far as his body or his mere power of mind is concerned. Man cannot come to Christ because his nature is so corrupt that he has neither the will nor the power to come to Christ unless drawn by the Spirit.

But let me give you a better illustration. You see a mother with her baby in her arms. You put a knife into her hand and tell her to stab that baby in the heart. She replies and very truthfully, "I cannot." Now, so far as her bodily power is concerned, she can if she pleases. There is the knife and there is the child. The child cannot resist and she has quite sufficient strength in her hand to immediately stab it. But she is quite correct when she says she cannot do it! As a mere act of the mind, it is quite possible she might think of such a thing as killing the child and yet she says she cannot think of such a thing. And she does not say falsely, for her nature as a mother forbids her doing a thing from which her soul revolts. Simply because she is that child's parent, she feels she cannot kill it. It is even so with a sinner. Coming to Christ is so obnoxious to human nature that although, as far as physical and mental forces are concerned, (and these have but a very narrow sphere in salvation), men could come if they would—it is strictly correct to say that they cannot and will not unless the Father who has sent Christ draws them! Let us enter a little more deeply into the subject and try to show you wherein this inability of man consists in its more minute particulars.

1. First it lies in the obstinacy of the human will. "Oh," says the Arminian, "men may be saved if they will." We reply, "My dear Sir, we all believe that. But it is just the if they will that is the difficulty. We assert that no man will come to Christ unless he is drawn. No, we do not assert it, but Christ Himself declares it—'You will not come unto Me that you might have life.' And as long as that, 'you will not come,' stands on record in Holy Scripture, Christ shall not be brought to believe in any doctrine of the freedom of the human will." It is strange how people, when talking about free will, talk of things which they do not at all understand. "Now" says one, "I believe men can be saved if they will." My dear Sir, that is not the question at all. The question is, are men ever found naturally willing to submit to the humbling terms of the Gospel of Christ? We declare, upon Scriptural authority, that the human will is so desperately set on mischief, so depraved and so inclined to everything that is evil—so disinclined to everything that is good—that without the powerful, supernatural, irresistible influence of the Holy Spirit, no human will will ever be constrained towards Christ! You reply that men sometimes are willing without the help of the Holy Spirit. I answer—did you ever meet with any person who was? Scores and hundreds, no, thousands of Christians have I conversed with, of different opinions, young and old—but it has never been my lot to meet with one who could affirm that he came to Christ of himself without being drawn. The universal confession of all true Believers is this—"I know that unless Jesus Christ had sought me when a stranger wandering from

the fold of God, I would to this very hour have been wandering far from Him—at a distance from Him—and loving that distance well." With common consent, all Believers affirm the Truth of God that men will not come to Christ till the Father who has sent Christ draws them!

2. Again, not only is the will obstinate, but the understanding is darkened. Of that we have abundant Scriptural proof. I am not now making mere assertions, but stating Doctrines authoritatively taught in the Holy Scriptures and known in the conscience of every Christian—that the understanding of man is so dark that he cannot by any means understand the things of God until his understanding has been opened! Man is by nature blind within. The Cross of Christ, so laden with glories and glittering with attractions, never attracts him because he is blind and cannot see its beauties. Talk to him of the wonders of the Creation. Show to him the many-colored arch that spans the sky. Let him behold the glories of a landscape—he is well able to see all these things. But talk to him of the wonders of the Covenant of Grace; speak to him of the security of the Believer in Christ; tell him of the beauties of the Person of the Redeemer and he is quite deaf to all your descriptions! You are as one that plays a goodly tune, it is true, but he regards not, he is deaf, he has no comprehension! Or, to return to the verse which we so specially marked in our reading, "The natural man receives not the things of the Spirit of God, for they are foolishness unto him: neither can he know them because they are spiritually discerned," and inasmuch as he is a natural man, it is

not in his power to discern the things of God. "Well," says one, "I think I have arrived at a very tolerable judgment in matters of theology. I think I understand almost every point." True, that you may do in the letter of it—but in the spirit of it, in the true reception thereof into the soul and in the actual understanding of it, it is impossible for you to have attained—unless you have been drawn by the Spirit! For as long as that Scripture stands true—that carnal men cannot receive spiritual things—it must be true that you have not received them unless you have been renewed and made a spiritual man in Christ Jesus. The will, then and the understanding, are two great doors, both blocked up against our coming to Christ! And until these are opened by the sweet influences of the Divine Spirit, they must be forever closed to anything like coming to Christ.

3. Again, the affections, which constitute a very great part of man, are depraved. Man, as he is, before he receives the Grace of God, loves anything and everything but spiritual things! If you need proof of this, look around you. There needs no monument to the depravity of the human affections. Cast your eyes everywhere—there is not a street, nor a house, no, nor a heart which does not bear upon it sad evidence of this dreadful truth! Why is it that men are not found on the Sabbath universally flocking to the House of God? Why are we not more constantly found reading our Bibles? How is it that prayer is a duty almost universally neglected? Why is it that Christ Jesus is so little loved? Why are even His professed followers so cold in their affections to Him? From where arise these things? Assuredly, dear Brothers

and Sisters, we can trace them to no other source than this—the corruption and vitiation of the affections! We love that which we ought to hate and we hate that which we ought to love! It is but human nature, fallen human nature—that man should love this present life better than the life to come. It is but the effect of the Fall that man should love sin better than righteousness and the ways of this world better than the ways of God. And again, we repeat it—until these affections are renewed and turned into a fresh channel by the gracious drawings of the Father, it is not possible for any man to love the Lord Jesus Christ!

4. Yet once more—conscience, too, has been overpowered by the Fall. I believe there is no more egregious mistake made by divines than when they tell people that conscience is the vicegerent of God within the soul and that it is one of those powers which retains its ancient dignity and stands erect amidst the fall of its compeers! My Brothers and Sisters, when man fell in the Garden, manhood entirely fell! There was not one single pillar in the temple of manhood that stood erect. It is true, conscience was not destroyed. The pillar was not shattered. It fell, and it fell in one piece and here it lies alone—the mightiest remnant of God's once perfect work in man! But that conscience is fallen, I am sure. Look at men. Who among them is the possessor of a "good conscience toward God," but the regenerated man? Do you imagine that if men's consciences always spoke loudly and clearly to them, they would live in the daily commission of acts which are as opposed to the right as darkness to light? No, Beloved—conscience

can tell me that I am a sinner, but conscience cannot make me feel that I am one! Conscience may tell me that such-and-such a thing is wrong, but how wrong it is, conscience itself does not know. Did any man's conscience, unenlightened by the Spirit, ever tell him that his sins deserved damnation? Or if conscience did do that, did it ever lead any man to feel an abhorrence of sin as sin? In fact, did conscience ever bring a man to such a self-renunciation that he did totally abhor himself and all his works and come to Christ? No, conscience, although it is not dead, is ruined! Its power is impaired; it has not that clearness of eye and that strength of hand and that thunder of voice which it had before the Fall. It has ceased, to a great degree, to exert its supremacy in the town of Mansoul. Then, Beloved, it becomes necessary for this very reason—because conscience is depraved—that the Holy Spirit should step in to show us our need of a Savior and draw us to the Lord Jesus Christ.

"Still," says one, "as far as you have so far gone, it appears to me that you consider that the reason why men do not come to Christ is that they will not, rather than they cannot." True, most true! I believe the greatest reason of man's inability is the obstinacy of his will. That once overcome, I think the great stone is rolled away from the sepulcher and the hardest part of the battle is already won. But allow me to go a little further. My text does not say, "No man will come," but it says, "No man can come." Now, many interpreters believe that the, can, here is but a strong expression conveying no more meaning than the word will. I feel assured that this is not correct. There is in man not only unwillingness to be saved, but there is a spiritual powerlessness to come to Christ. And this I will prove to every Christian, at any rate. Beloved, I speak to you who have already been quickened by Divine Grace. Does not your experience teach you that there are times when you have a will to serve God and yet have not the power? Have you not sometimes been obliged to say that you have wished to believe but you have had to pray, "Lord, help my unbelief"? Because, although willing enough to receive God's Testimony, your own carnal nature was too strong for you and you felt you needed supernatural help. Are you able to go into your room at any hour you choose and to fall upon your knees and say, "Now, it is my will that I should be very earnest in prayer and that I should draw near unto God"? I ask, do you find your power equal to your will? You could say, even at the bar of God Himself, that you are sure you are not mistaken in your willingness. You are willing to be wrapped up in devotion. It is your will that your soul should not wander from a pure contemplation of the Lord Jesus Christ—but you find that you cannot do that, even when you are willing—without the help of the Spirit of God! Now, if the quickened child of God finds a spiritual inability, how much more the sinner who is dead in trespasses and sin? If even the advanced Christian, after 30 or 40 years, finds himself sometimes willing and yet powerless—if such is his experience—does it not seem more than likely that the poor sinner who has not yet believed should find a need of strength as well as a need of will?

But, again, there is another argument. If the sinner has strength to come to Christ, I should like to know how we are to understand those continual descriptions of the sinner's state which we meet with in God's Holy Word? Now, a sinner is said to be dead in trespasses and sins. Will you affirm that death implies nothing more than the absence of a will? Surely a corpse is quite as unable as unwilling. Or again, do not all men see that there is a distinction between will and power? Might not that corpse be sufficiently quickened to get a will and yet be so powerless that it could not lift as much as its hand or foot? Have we ever seen cases in which persons have been just sufficiently re-animated to give evidence of life—and have yet been so near death that they could not have performed the slightest action? Is there not a clear difference between the giving of the will and the giving of power? It is quite certain, however, that where the will is given, the power will follow. Make a man willing and he shall be made powerful, for when God gives the will, He does not tantalize man by giving him to wish for that which he is unable to do! Nevertheless He makes such a division between the will and the power that it shall be seen that both things are quite distinct gifts of the Lord God.

Then I must ask one more question. If that were all that were needed to make a man willing, do you not at once degrade the Holy Spirit? Are we not in the habit of giving all the Glory of salvation worked in us to God the Spirit? But now, if all that God the Spirit does for me is to make me willing to do these things for myself, am I not in a great measure a sharer with the Holy

Spirit in the Glory? And may I not boldly stand up and say, "It is true the Spirit gave me the will to do it, but still I did it myself and therein will I glory, for if I did these things myself without assistance from on high, I will not cast my crown at His feet! It is my own crown, I earned it and I will keep it." Inasmuch as the Holy Spirit is evermore in Scripture set forth as the Person who works in us to will and to do of His own good pleasure, we hold it to be a legitimate inference that He must do something more for us than the mere making of us willing. Therefore there must be another thing besides need of will in a sinner—there must be absolute and actual need of power.

Now, before I leave this statement, let me address myself to you for a moment. I am often charged with preaching Doctrines that may do a great deal of hurt. Well, I shall not deny the charge, for I am not careful to answer in this matter. I have my witnesses here present to prove that the things which I have preached have done a great deal of hurt, but they have not done hurt either to morality or to God's Church. The hurt has been on the side of Satan! There are not ones or twos but many hundreds who this morning rejoice that they have been brought near to God. From having been profane Sabbath-breakers, drunkards, or worldly persons, they have been brought to know and love the Lord Jesus Christ. And if this is any hurt, may God in His infinite mercy send us a thousand times as much! But further, what Truth is there in the world which will not hurt a man who chooses to make hurt of it? You who preach general redemption are very fond of proclaiming the great Truth of God's mercy to the last moment. But how dare you preach that? Many people make hurt of it by putting off the Day of Grace and thinking that the last hour may do as well as the first. Why, if we ever preached anything which man could misuse, and abuse, we must hold our tongues forever! Still says one, "Well then, if I cannot save myself, and cannot come to Christ, I must sit still and do nothing." If men say so, on their own heads shall be their doom! We have very plainly told you that there are many things you can do! To be found continually in the House of God is in your power. To study the Word of God with diligence is in your power. To renounce your outward sin, to forsake the vices in which you indulge, to make your life honest, sober and righteous is in your power. For these you need no help from the Holy Spirit. All these you can do yourself. But to truly come to Christ is not in your power until you are renewed by the Holy Spirit! And mark you, your lack of power is no excuse, seeing that you have no desire to come and are living in willful rebellion against God! Your lack of power lies mainly in the obstinacy of your nature.

Suppose a liar says that it is not in his power to speak the truth, that he has been a liar so long that he cannot leave it off? Is that an excuse for him? Suppose a man who has long indulged in lust should tell you that he finds his lusts have so girt about him like a great iron net that he cannot get rid of them? Would you take that as an excuse? Truly it is none at all! If a drunkard has become so foully a drunk that he finds it impossible to pass a public bar without stepping in, do you therefore excuse him? No, because his inability to reform lies in his nature—which he has no desire to restrain or conquer. The thing that is done and the thing that causes the thing that is done—being both from the root of sin—are two evils which cannot excuse each other. It is because you have learned to do evil that you cannot now learn to do well and instead, therefore, of letting you sit down to excuse yourselves—let me put a thunderbolt beneath the seat of your sloth—that you may be startled by it and awakened! Remember, that to sit still is to be damned to all eternity! Oh, that God the Holy Spirit might make use of this Truth of God in a very different manner! Before I have done, I trust I shall be enabled to show you how it is that this Truth, which apparently condemns men and shuts them out, is, after all, the great Truth of God which has been blessed to the conversion of men!

II. Our second point is THE FATHER'S DRAWINGS. "No man can come to Me except the Father who sent Me draws him." How, then, does the Father draw men? Arminian divines generally say that God draws men by the preaching of the Gospel. Very true. The preaching of the Gospel is the instrument of drawing men, but there must be something more than this. Let me ask to whom did Christ address these words? Why, to the people of Capernaum, where he had often preached, where he had mournfully and plaintively uttered the woes of the Law and the invitations of the Gospel! In that city He had done many mighty works and worked many miracles! In fact, such teaching and such miraculous attestation had He given to them that He declared that Tyre and Sidon would have repented long ago in sackcloth and ashes if they had been blessed with such privileges! Now if the preaching of Christ, Himself, did not avail to the enabling these men to come to Christ, it cannot be possible that all that was intended by the drawing of the Father was simply preaching. No, Brothers and Sisters, you must note again—He does not say no man can come except the minister draws him, but except the Father draws him! Now there is such a thing as being drawn by the Gospel and drawn by the minister without being drawn by God. Clearly it is a Divine drawing that is meant, a drawing by the Most High God—the First Person of the most glorious Trinity sending out the Third Person, the Holy Spirit, to induce men to come to Christ! Another person turns around and says with a sneer, "Then do you think that Christ drags men to Himself, seeing that they are unwilling!" I remember meeting once with a man who said to me, "Sir, you preach that Christ takes people by the hair of their heads and drags them to Himself." I asked him whether he could refer to the date of the sermon wherein I preached that extraordinary doctrine, for if he could, I should be very much obliged. However, he could not. But said I, while Christ does not drag people to Himself by the hair of their heads, I believe that He draws them by the heart quite as powerfully as your caricature would suggest! Mark that in the Father's drawing there is no compulsion whatever. Christ never compelled any man to come to Him against his will. If a man is unwilling to be saved, Christ does not save him against his will!

How, then, does the Holy Spirit draw him? Why, by making him willing. It is true He does not use "moral persuasion." He knows a better method of reaching the heart. He goes to the secret fountain of the heart and he knows how, by some mysterious operation, to turn the will in an opposite direction, so that, as Ralph Erskine paradoxically puts it, the man is saved "with full consent against his will," that is, against his old will he is saved! But he is saved with full consent for he is made willing in the day of God's power. Do not imagine that any man will go to Heaven kicking and struggling all the way against the hand that draws him. Do not conceive that any man will be plunged in the bath of a Savior's blood while he is striving to run away from the Savior. Oh, no! It is quite true that first of all man is unwilling to be saved. When the Holy Spirit has put His influence into the heart, the text is fulfilled—"draw me and I will run after You." We follow on while He draws us, glad to obey the voice which once we had despised. But the gist of the matter lies in the turning of the will. How that is done no flesh knows. It is one of those mysteries that is clearly perceived as a fact, but the cause of which no tongue can tell and no heart can guess. The apparent way, however, in which the Holy Spirit operates, we can tell you. The first thing the Holy Spirit does when He comes into a man's heart is this—He finds him with a very good opinion of himself. And there is nothing which prevents a man coming to

Christ like a good opinion of himself. "Why," says man, "I don't want to come to Christ. I have as good a righteousness as anybody can desire. I feel I can walk into Heaven on my own rights!" The Holy Spirit lays bare his heart—lets him see the loathsome cancer that is there eating away his life—uncovers to him all the blackness and defilement of that sink of Hell, the human heart. Then the man stands aghast, "I never thought I was like this! Oh, those sins I thought were little have swelled out to an immense stature. What I thought was a molehill has grown into a mountain! It was but the hyssop on the wall before, but now it has become a cedar of Lebanon. Oh," says the man within himself, "I will try and reform. I will do good deeds enough to wash these black deeds out."

Then comes the Holy Spirit and shows him that he cannot do this. He takes away all his fancied power and strength, so that the man falls down on his knees in agony and cries, "Oh, once I thought I could save myself by my good works, but now I find that—

Could my tears forever flow,
Could my zeal no respite know,
All for sin could not atone,
You must save and You alone!"

Then the heart sinks and the man is ready to despair. And he says, "I never can be saved. Nothing can save me." Then comes the Holy Spirit and shows the sinner the Cross of Christ, gives him eyes anointed with heavenly eye-salve and says, "Look to yonder Cross. That Man died to save sinners. You feel that you are a sinner. He died to save you." And He enables the heart to believe and to come to Christ—and when it comes to Christ by this sweet drawing of the Spirit, it finds "a peace with God which passes all understanding, which keeps his heart and mind through Jesus Christ our Lord." Now, you will plainly perceive that all this may be done without any compulsion. Man is as much drawn willingly, as if he were not drawn at all. And he comes to Christ with full consent, with as full a consent as if no secret influence had ever been exercised in his heart. But that influence must be exercised or else there never has been and there never will be any man who either can or will come to the Lord Jesus Christ!

III. And now we gather up our ends and conclude by trying to make a practical application of the Doctrine—and, we trust, a comfortable one. "Well," says one "if what this man preaches is true, what is to become of my religion? For do you know I have been a long while trying and I do not like to hear you say a man cannot save himself. I believe he can and I mean to persevere. But if I am to believe what you say, I must give it all up and begin again." My dear Friends, it will be a very happy thing if you do. Do not think that I shall be at all alarmed if you do so! Remember, what you are doing is building your house upon sand and it is but an act of charity if I can shake it a little for you. Let me assure you, in God's name, if your religion has no better foundation than your own strength, it will not stand at the bar of God! Nothing will last to eternity but that which came from eternity! Unless the Everlasting God has done a good work in your heart, all you may have done must be unraveled at the last day of account. It is all in vain for you to be a Church-goer or Chapel-goer, a good keeper of the Sabbath, an observer of your prayers. It is all in vain for you to be honest to your neighbors and reputable in your conversation. If you hope to be saved by these things, it is all in vain for you to trust in them! Go on—be as honest as you like. Keep the Sabbath perpetually; be as holy as you can. I would not dissuade you from these things. God forbid! Grow in them, but oh, do not trust in them! For if you rely upon these things you will find they will fail you when most you need them. And if there is anything else that you have found yourself able to do unassisted by Divine Grace, the sooner you can get rid of the hope that has been engendered by it, the better for you—for it is a foul delusion to rely upon anything that flesh can do!

A spiritual Heaven must be inhabited by spiritual men and preparation for it must be worked by the Spirit of God. "Well," cries another, "I have been sitting under a ministry where I have been told that I could, at my own option, repent and believe and the consequence is that I have been putting it off from day to day. I thought I could come one day as well as another. That I had only to say, 'Lord, have mercy upon me,' and believe, and then I should be saved. Now you have taken all this hope away for me, Sir. I feel amazement and horror taking hold upon me." Again, I say, "My dear Friend, I am very glad of it! This was the effect which I hoped to produce by God's Grace. I pray that you may feel this a great deal more. When you have no hope of saving yourself, I shall have hope that God has begun to save you! As soon as you say, "Oh, I cannot come to Christ. Lord, draw me, help me," I shall rejoice over you! He who has got a will, though he has not power, has Grace begun in his heart and God will not leave him until the work is finished! But, careless Sinner, learn that your salvation now hangs in God's hands! Oh, remember you are entirely in the hands of God. You have sinned against Him and if He wills to damn you, damned you are! You can not resist His will nor thwart His purpose. You have deserved His wrath and if He chooses to pour the full shower of that wrath upon your head, you can do nothing to reverse it. If, on the other hand, He chooses to save you, He is able to save you to the very uttermost! But you lie as much in His hands as the summer's moth beneath your own fingers. He is the God whom you are grieving every day. Does it not make you tremble to think that your eternal destiny now hangs upon the will of Him whom you have angered and incensed? Does not this make your knees knock together and your blood curdle? If it does so, I rejoice, inasmuch as this may be the first effect of the Spirit's drawing in your soul. Oh, tremble to think that the God whom you have angered is the God upon whom your salvation or your condemnation entirely depends! Tremble and "kiss the Son lest He be angry and you perish from the way while His wrath is kindled but a little."

Now, the comfortable reflection is this—some of you this morning are conscious that you are coming to Christ. Have you not begun to weep the penitential tear? Did not your closet witness your prayerful preparation for the hearing of the Word of God? And during the service this morning, has not your heart said within you, "Lord, save me, or I perish, for save myself I cannot"? And could you not now stand up in your seat and sing—

"Oh, Sovereign Grace my heart subdue!
I would be led in triumph, too,
A willing captive of my Lord,
To sing the triumph of His Word"?

And have I not myself heard you say in your heart—"Jesus, Jesus, my whole trust is in You. I know that no righteousness of my own can save me, but only You. O Christ—sink or swim, I cast myself on You"? Oh, my Brothers and Sisters, you are drawn by the Father, for you could not have come unless He had drawn you! Sweet thought! And if He has drawn you, do you know what is the delightful inference? Let me repeat just one text, and may that comfort you—"The Lord has appeared of old unto me, saying, I have loved you with an everlasting love—therefore with loving kindness have I drawn you." Yes, my poor weeping Brothers and Sisters, inasmuch as you are now coming to Christ, God has drawn you! And inasmuch as He has drawn you, it is a proof that He has loved you from before the foundation of the world! Let your heart leap within you, you are one of His! Your name was written on the Savior's hands when they were nailed to the accursed tree. Your name glitters on the breastplate of the great High Priest today. And it was there before the daystar knew its place, or planets ran their round.

Rejoice in the Lord, you who have come to Christ, and shout for joy all you who have been drawn of the Father! For this is your proof—your solemn testimony—

that you from among men have been chosen in eternal election and that you shall be kept by the power of God, through faith, unto the salvation which is ready to be revealed!

Sermons No.s 41, 42
Delivered on September 2nd, 1855
by Rev. C. H. Spurgeon
at New Park Street Chapel, Southwark

UNCONDITIONAL ELECTION

"But we are bound to give thanks always to God for you, brethren beloved of the Lord, because God has from the beginning chosen you to salvation through sanctification of the Spirit and belief of the truth: Whereunto He called you by our Gospel, to the obtaining of the glory of our Lord Jesus Christ."

—2 Thessalonians 2:13,14

IF there were no other text in the Sacred Word except this one I think we should all be bound to receive and acknowledge the truthfulness of the great and glorious doctrine of God's ancient choice of His family. But there seems to be an inveterate prejudice in the human mind against this doctrine—and although most other doctrines will be received by professing Christians, some with caution, others with pleasure—this one seems to be most frequently disregarded and discarded. In many of our pulpits it would be reckoned a high sin and treason to preach a sermon upon election because they could not make it what they call a "practical" discourse.

I believe they have erred from the truth. Whatever God has revealed He has revealed for a purpose. There is nothing in Scripture which may not, under the influence of God's Spirit, be turned into a practical discourse—"for all Scripture is given by inspiration of God and is profitable" for some purpose of spiritual usefulness. It is true, it may not be turned into a free will discourse—that we know right well—but it can be turned into a practical free grace discourse. And free grace practice is the best practice when the true doctrines of God's immutable love are brought to bear upon the hearts of saints and sinners. Now, I trust this morning some of you who are startled at the very sound of this word will say, "I will give it a fair hearing. I will lay aside my prejudices, I will just hear what this man has to say."

Do not shut your ears and say at once, "It is high doctrine." Who has authorized you to call it high or low? Why should you oppose yourself to God's doctrine? Remember what became of the children who found fault with God's Prophet and exclaimed, "Go up, you bald-head; go up, you bald-head." Say nothing against God's doctrines, lest haply some evil beast should come out of the forest and devour you, also. There are other woes beside the open judgment of Heaven—take heed that these fall not on your head. Lay aside your prejudices—listen calmly, listen dispassionately—hear what Scripture says.

And when you receive the truth, if God should be pleased to reveal and manifest it to your souls, do not be ashamed to confess it. To confess you were wrong yesterday is only to acknowledge that you are a little wiser today. Instead of being a reflection on yourself, it is an honor to your judgment and shows that you are improving in the knowledge of the Truth of God. Do not be ashamed to learn and to cast aside your old doctrines and views. But take up that which you may more plainly see to be in the Word of God. And if you do not see it to be here in the Bible—whatever I may say, or whatever authorities I may plead—I beseech you, as you love your souls, reject it. And if from this pulpit you ever hear things contrary to this Sacred Word, remember that the Bible must be first and God's minister must lie underneath it.

We must not stand on the Bible to preach—we must preach with the Bible above our heads. After all we have preached, we are well aware that the mountain of truth is higher than our eyes can discern—clouds and darkness are round about its summit and we cannot discern its topmost pinnacle. Yet we will try to preach it as well as we can. But since we are mortal and liable to err, exercise your judgment—"Try the spirits, whether they are of God"—and if on mature reflection on your bended knees you are led to disregard election—a thing which I consider to be utterly impossible—then forsake it. Do not hear it preached, but believe and confess whatever you see to be God's Word. I can say no more than that by way of introduction.

Now, first. I shall speak a little concerning the truthfulness of this doctrine—"God has from the beginning chosen you to salvation." Secondly, I shall try to prove that this election is absolute—"He has from the beginning chosen you to salvation," not for sanctification, but "through sanctification of the Spirit and belief of the truth." Thirdly, this election is eternal because the text says, "God has from the beginning chosen you." Fourthly, it is personal—"He has chosen you."

Then we will look at the effects of the doctrine—see what it does. And lastly, as God may enable us, we will try and look at its tendencies and see whether it is indeed a terrible and licentious doctrine. We will take the flower and like true bees, see whether there is any honey whatever in it—whether any good can come of it—or whether it is an unmixed, undiluted evil.

I. First, I must try and prove that the doctrine is TRUE. And let me begin with an argumentum ad hominen—I will speak to you according to your different positions and stations. There are some of you who belong to the Church of England and I am happy to see so many of you here. Though now and then I certainly say some very hard things about Church and State, yet I love the old Church, for she has in her communion many godly ministers and eminent saints. Now I know you are great Believers in what the Articles declare to be sound doctrine. I will give you a specimen of what they utter concerning election, so that if you believe them, you cannot avoid receiving election. I will read a portion of the 17th Article upon Predestination and Election:

"Predestination to life is the everlasting purpose of God, whereby (before the foundations of the world were laid) He has continually decreed by His counsel secret to us, to deliver from curse and damnation those whom He has chosen in Christ out of mankind and to bring them by Christ to everlasting salvation, as vessels made to honor. Wherefore they which are endued with so excellent a benefit of God are called according to God's purpose by His Spirit working in due season: they through grace obey the calling: they are justified freely: they are made sons of God by adoption: they are made like the image of His only-begotten Son Jesus Christ: they walk religiously in good works and at length, by God's mercy, they attain to everlasting felicity."

Now, I think any Churchman, if he is a sincere and honest believer in Mother Church, must be a thorough believer in election. True, if he turns to certain other portions of the Prayer Book, he will find things contrary to the doctrines of free grace and altogether apart from Scriptural teaching. But if he looks at the Articles, he must see that God has chosen His people unto eternal life. I am not so desperately enamored, however, of that book as you may be—and I have only used this Article to show you that if you belong to the Establishment of England you should at least offer no objection to this doctrine of predestination.

Another human authority whereby I would confirm the doctrine of election is the old Waldensian Creed. If you read the creed of the old Waldenses—emanating from them in the midst of the burning heat of persecution—you will see that these renowned professors and confessors of the Christian faith did most firmly receive and embrace this doctrine as being a portion of the Truth of God. I have copied from an old book one of the Articles of their faith: "That God saves from corruption and damnation those whom He has chosen from the foundations of the world, not for any disposition, faith, or holiness that before saw in them, but of His mere mercy in Christ Jesus His Son, passing by all the rest according to the irreprehensible reason of His own free will and justice."

It is no novelty, then, that I am preaching no new doctrine. I love to proclaim these strong old doctrines which are called by nickname Calvinism but which are surely and verily the revealed Truth of God as it is in Christ Jesus. By this truth I make a pilgrimage into the past and as I go I see father after father, confessor after confessor, martyr after martyr, standing up to shake hands with me. Were I a Pelagian, or a believer in the doctrine of free will, I should have to walk for centuries all alone. Here and there a heretic of no very honorable character might rise up and call me Brother. But taking these things to be the standard of my faith, I see the land of the ancients peopled with my Brothers and Sisters—I behold multitudes who confess the same as I do and acknowledge that this is the religion of God's own Church.

I also give you an extract from the old Baptist Confession. We are Baptists in this congregation—the greater part of us at any rate—and we like to see what our own forefathers wrote. Some two hundred years ago the Baptists assembled together and published their articles of faith to put an end to certain reports against their orthodoxy which had gone forth to the world. I turn to this old book—which I have just published—Baptist Confession of Faith—and I find the following as the 3rd Article: "By the decree of God for the manifestation of

His glory some men and angels are predestinated, or foreordained to eternal life through Jesus Christ to the praise of His glorious grace. Others being left to act in their sin to their just condemnation to the praise of His glorious justice. These angels and men thus predestinated and foreordained, are particularly and unchangeably designed and their number so certain and definite that it cannot be either increased or diminished. Those of mankind that are predestinated to life, God, before the foundation of the world was laid, according to His eternal and immutable purpose and the secret counsel and good pleasure of His will, has chosen in Christ unto everlasting glory out of His mere free grace and love, without any other thing in the creature as condition or cause moving Him hereunto."

As for these human authorities, I care not one rush for all three of them. I care not what they say, pro or con, as to this doctrine. I have only used them as a kind of confirmation to your faith, to show you that while I may be railed upon as a heretic and as a hyper-Calvinist, after all I am backed up by antiquity. All the past stands by me. I do not care for the present. Give me the past and I will hope for the future. Let the present rise up in my teeth, I will not care. What though a host of the Churches of London may have forsaken the great cardinal doctrines of God, it matters not. If a handful of us stand alone in an unflinching maintenance of the sovereignty of our God, if we are beset by enemies, yes, and even by our own Brothers and Sisters who ought to be our friends and helpers, it matters not—if we can but count upon the past—the noble army of martyrs, the glorious host of confessors. They are our friends. They are the witnesses of truth and they stand by us. With these for us, we will not say that we stand alone, but we may exclaim, "Lo, God has reserved unto Himself seven thousand that have not bowed the knee unto Baal." But the best of all is—God is with us!

The great Truth of God is always the Bible and the Bible alone. My Hearers, you do not believe in any other book than the Bible, do you? If I could prove this from all the books in Christendom—if I could fetch back the Alexandrian library and prove it there—you would not believe it any more. But you surely will believe what is in God's Word. I have selected a few texts to read to you. I love to give you a whole volley of texts when I am afraid you will distrust a truth so that you may be too astonished to doubt, if you do not in reality believe. Just let me run through a catalogue of passages where the people of God are called elect. Of course if the people are called elect, there must be election. If Jesus Christ and His Apostles were accustomed to call Believers by the title of elect, we must certainly believe that they were so, otherwise the term does not mean anything. Jesus Christ says, "Except that the Lord had shortened those days, no flesh should be saved; but for the elect's sake, whom He has chosen, He has shortened the days."

"False Christs and false prophets shall rise and shall show signs and wonders, to seduce, if it were possible, even the elect." "Then shall He send His angels and shall gather together His elect from the four winds, from the uttermost parts of the earth to the uttermost part of

Heaven." (Mark 13:20, 22, 27) "Shall not God avenge His own elect who cry day and night unto Him, though He bear long with them?" (Luke 18:7) Together with many other passages which might be selected, wherein either the word "elect," or "chosen," or "foreordained," or "appointed," is mentioned—or the phrase "My sheep," or some similar designation, showing that Christ's people are distinguished from the rest of mankind.

But you have concordances and I will not trouble you with texts. Throughout the Epistles the saints are constantly called "the elect." In the Colossians we find Paul saying, "Put on therefore, as the elect of God, holy and beloved, bowels of mercies." When he writes to Titus, he calls himself, "Paul, a servant of God and an Apostle of Jesus Christ, according to the faith of God's elect." Peter says, "Elect according to the foreknowledge of God the Father." Then if you turn to John, you will find he is very fond of the word. He says, "The elder to the elect lady." And he speaks of our "elect sister." And we know where it is written, "The church that is at Babylon, elected together with you."

They were not ashamed of the word in those days. They were not afraid to talk about it. Nowadays the word has been dressed up with diversities of meaning and persons have mutilated and marred the doctrine so that they have made it a very doctrine of devils. I do confess that many who call themselves Believers have gone to rank Antinomianism. But not withstanding this, why should I be ashamed of it, if men wrest it? We love God's Truth on the rack as well as when it is walking upright. If there were a martyr whom we loved before he came on the rack we should love him more still when he was stretched there.

When God's Truth is stretched on the rack, we do not call it falsehood. We love not to see it racked but we love it even when racked because we can discern what its proper proportions ought to have been if it had not been racked and tortured by the cruelty and inventions of men. If you will read many of the Epistles of the ancient fathers you will find them always writing to the people of God as the "elect." Indeed the common conversational term used among many of the Churches by the primitive Christians to one another was that of the "elect." They would often use the term to one another showing that it was generally believed that all God's people were manifestly "elect."

But now for the verses that will positively prove the doctrine. Open your Bibles and turn to John 15:16 and there you will see that Jesus Christ has chosen His people, for He says, "You have not chosen Me, but I have chosen you and ordained you, that you should go and bring forth fruit and that your fruit should remain: that whatsoever you shall ask of the Father in My name, He may give it you." Then in the 19th verse, "If you were of the world, the world would love his own, but because you are not of the world, but I have chosen you out of the world, therefore the world hates you." Then in the 17th chapter and the 8th and 9 th verses, "For I have given unto them the words which You gave Me; and they have received them and have known surely that I came out from You and they have believed that You did send Me. I pray for them: I pray not for the world, but for them which You have given Me for they are Yours."

Turn to Acts 13:48: "And when the Gentiles heard this, they were glad and glorified the Word of the Lord; and as many as were ordained to eternal life believed." They may try to split that passage into hairs if they like—but it says, "ordained to eternal life" in the original as plainly as it possibly can. And we do not care about all the different commentaries thereupon. You scarcely need to be reminded of Romans 8, because I trust you are all well-acquainted with that chapter and understand it by this time. In the 29th and following verses, it says, "For whom He did foreknow, He also did predestinate to be conformed to the image of His Son, that He might be the firstborn among many Brethren. Moreover, whom He did predestinate, them He also called: and whom He called, them He also justified and whom He justified, them He also glorified. What shall we then say to these things? If God is for us, who can be against us? He that spared not His own Son, but delivered Him up for us all, how shall He not with Him also freely give us all things? Who shall lay anything to the charge of God's elect?"

It would also be unnecessary to repeat the whole of the 9th chapter of Romans. As long as that remains in the Bible, no man shall be able to prove Arminianism. So long as that is written there, not the most violent contortions of the passage will ever be able to exterminate the doctrine of election from the Scriptures. Let us read such verses as these—"For the children being not yet born, neither having done any good or evil, that the purpose of God according to election might stand, not of works, but of Him that calls; it was said unto her, The elder shall serve the younger." Then read the 22nd verse, "What if God, willing to show His wrath and to make His power known, endured with much longsuffering the vessels of wrath fitted to destruction? And that He might make known the riches of His glory on the vessels of mercy, which He had afore prepared unto glory?"

Then go on to Romans 11:7—"What then? Israel has not obtained that which he seeks for; but the election has obtained it and the rest were blinded." In the 6 th verse of the same chapter, we read—"Even so then at this present time also there is a remnant according to the election of grace." You, no doubt, all recollect the passage in 1 Corinthians 1:26-29: "For you see your calling, Brethren, how that not many wise men after the flesh, not many mighty, not many noble are called: but God has chosen the foolish things of the world to confound the wise; and God has chosen the weak things of the world to confound the things which are mighty; and base things of the world and things which are despised, has God chosen, yes and things which are not, to bring to nothing things which are: that no flesh should glory in His presence."

Again, remember the verse in 1Thessalonians 5:9—"God has not appointed us to wrath, but to obtain salvation by our Lord Jesus Christ," and then you have my text, which should be quite enough. But, if you need any more, you can find them at your leisure if we have not quite removed your suspicions as to the doctrine not being true. Methinks, my Friends, that this overwhelming mass of Scripture testimony must stagger those who dare to laugh at this doctrine. What shall we say of those who have so often despised it and denied its Divinity? What shall we say to those who have railed at its justice and dared to defy God and call Him an Almighty tyrant, when they have heard of His having elected so many to eternal life? Can you, O Rejecter, cast it out of the Bible? Can you take the penknife of Jehudi and cut it out of the Word of God?

Would you be like the women at the feet of Solomon and have the child rent in halves that you might have your half? Is it not here in Scripture? And is it not your duty to bow before it and meekly acknowledge what you understand not—to receive it as the Truth even though you could not understand its meaning? I will not attempt to prove the justice of God in having thus elected some and left others. It is not for me to vindicate my Master. He will speak for Himself and He does so—"But, O man, who are you that replies against God? Shall the thing formed say to Him that formed it, Why have you made me thus? Has not the potter power over the clay of the same lump to make one vessel unto honor and another unto dishonor?" Who is he that shall say unto his father, "What have you begotten? . . . or unto his mother, "What have you brought forth?" "I am the Lord—I form the light and create darkness. I, the Lord, do all these things. Who are you that replies against God? Tremble and kiss His rod; bow down and submit to His scepter; impugn not His justice and arraign not His acts before your bar, O man!"

But there are some who say, "It is hard for God to choose some and leave others." Now, I will ask you one question. Is there any of you here this morning who wishes to be holy, who wishes to be regenerate, to leave off sin and walk in holiness? "Yes, there is," says someone, "I do." Then God has elected you. But another says, "No. I don't want to be holy. I don't want to give up my lusts and my vices." Why should you grumble, then, that God has not elected you? For if you were elected you would not like it, according to your own confession. If God this morning had chosen you to holiness, you say you would not care for it. Do you not acknowledge that you prefer drunkenness to sobriety, dishonesty to honesty? You love this world's pleasures better than religion—then why should you grumble that God has not chosen you to religion?

If you love religion, He has chosen you to it. If you desire it, He has chosen you to it. If you do not, what right have you to say that God ought to have given you what you do not wish for? Supposing I had in my hand something which you do not value and I said I shall give it to such-and-such a person—you would have no right to grumble that I did not give it to you. You could not be so foolish as to grumble that the other has got what you do not care about. According to your own confession many of you do not want religion—do not want a new heart and a right spirit—do not want the forgiveness of sins. You do not want sanctification. You do not want to be elected to these things—then why should you grumble?

You count these things but as husks and why should you complain of God who has given them to those whom He has chosen? If you believe them to be good and desire them, they are there for you. God gives liberally to all those who desire—but first of all He makes them desire—otherwise they never would. If you love these things, He has elected you to them and you may have them. But if you do not, who are you that you should find fault with God when it is your own desperate will that keeps you from loving these things? Suppose a man in the street should say, "What a shame it is I cannot have a seat in the Chapel to hear what this man has to say." And suppose he says, "I hate the preacher—I can't bear his doctrine—but still it's a shame I have not a seat."

Would you expect a man to say so? No—you would at once say, "That man does not care for it. Why should he trouble himself about other people having what they value and he despises?" You do not like holiness, you do not like righteousness. If God has elected me to these things, has He hurt you by it? "Ah, but," say some, "I thought it meant that God elected some to Heaven and some to Hell." That is a very different matter from the Gospel doctrine. He has elected men to holiness and to righteousness and through that to Heaven. You must not say that He has elected these simply to Heaven and others only to Hell. He has elected you to holiness if you love holiness. If any of you love to be saved by Jesus Christ—Jesus Christ elected you to be saved. If any of you desire to have salvation you are elected to have it—if you desire it sincerely and earnestly. But, if you don't desire it, why on earth should you be so preposterously foolish as to grumble because God gives that, which you do not like, to other people?

II. Thus I have tried to say something with regard to the Truth of the doctrine of election. And now, briefly, let me say that election is absolute, that is, it does not depend upon what we are. The text says, "God has from the beginning chosen us unto salvation." But our opponents say that God chooses people because they are good—that He chooses them on account of sundry works which they have done. Now, we ask in reply to this, what works are those on account of which God elects His people? Are they what we commonly call "works of Law"?—works of obedience which the creature can render? If so, we reply to you—If men cannot be justified by the works of the Law, it seems to us pretty clear that they cannot be elected by the works of the Law. If they cannot be justified by their good deeds, they cannot be saved by them.

Then the decree of election could not have been formed upon good works. "But," say others, "God elected them on the foresight of their faith." Now God gives faith, therefore He could not have elected them on account of faith which He foresaw. There shall be twenty beggars in the street and I determine to give one of them a shilling. Will anyone say that I determined to give that one a shilling—that I elected him to have the shilling—because I foresaw that he would have it? That would be talking nonsense.

In like manner to say that God elected men because He foresaw they would have faith—which is salvation in the germ—would be too absurd for us to listen to for a moment. Faith is the gift of God. Every virtue comes from Him. Therefore it cannot have caused Him to elect men, because it is His gift. Election, we are sure, is absolute and altogether apart from the virtues which the saints have afterwards. What if a saint should be as holy and devout as Paul? What if he should be as bold as Peter, or as loving as John? Still he could claim nothing but what he received from his Maker.

I never knew a saint yet of any denomination who thought that God saved him because He foresaw that he would have these virtues and merits. Now, my Brethren, the best jewels that the saint ever wears, if they are jewels of our own fashioning, are not of the first water. There is something of earth mixed with them. The highest grace we ever possess has something of earthliness about it. We feel this when we are most refined, when we are most sanctified and our language must always be—

"I the chief of sinners am;
Jesus died for me."

Our only hope, our only plea, still hangs on grace as exhibited in the Person of Jesus Christ. And I am sure we must utterly reject and disregard all thought that our graces, which are gifts of our Lord, which are His right hand planting, could have ever caused His love. And we ever must sing—

"What was there in us that could merit esteem
Or give the Creator delight?
It was even so, Father, we ever must sing,
Because it seemed good in Your sight"

"He will have mercy on whom He will have mercy." He saves because He will save. And if you ask me why He saves me, I can only say because He would do it. Is there anything in me that should recommend me to God? No. I lay aside everything. I had nothing to recommend me. When God saved me I was the most abject, lost and ruined of the race. I lay before Him as an infant in my blood. Verily, I had no power to help myself. O how wretched did I feel and know myself to be! It you had something to recommend you to God, I never had. I will be content to be saved by grace, unalloyed, pure grace. I can boast of no merits. If you can do so, still I cannot. I must sing—

> **"Free grace alone from the first to the last**
> **Has won my affection and held my soul fast."**

III. Then, thirdly, this election is ETERNAL. "God has from the beginning chosen you unto eternal life." Can any man tell me when the beginning was? Years ago we thought the beginning of this world was when Adam came upon it. But we have discovered that thousands of years before that God was preparing chaotic matter to make it a fit abode for man, putting races of creatures upon it who might die and leave behind the marks of His handiwork and marvelous skill before He tried His hand on man. But that was not the beginning, for Revelation points us to a period long before this world was fashioned—to the days when the morning stars were begotten—when, like drops of dew, from the fingers of the morning stars and constellations fell trickling from the hand of God. When, by His own lips, He launched forth ponderous orbs. When with His own hand He sent comets, like thunderbolts, wandering through the sky to find one day their proper sphere.

We go back to years gone by, when worlds were made and systems fashioned, but we have not even approached the beginning yet. Until we go to the time when all the universe slept in the mind of God as yet unborn—until we enter the eternity where God the Creator lived alone, everything sleeping within Him, all creation resting in His mighty gigantic thought—we have not guessed the beginning. We may go back, back, back, ages upon ages. We may go back, if we might use such strange words, whole eternities and yet never arrive at the beginning. Our wings might be tired, our imagination would die away. Could it outstrip the lightnings flashing in majesty, power and rapidity, it would soon weary itself before it could get to the beginning.

But God from the beginning chose His people. When the unnavigated ether was yet unfanned by the wing of a single angel, when space was shoreless, or else unborn when universal silence reigned and not a voice or whisper shocked the solemnity of silence. When there was no being and no motion, no time and nothing but God Himself, alone in His eternity—when without the song of an angel, without the attendance of even the cherubim—long before the living creatures were born, or the wheels of the chariot of Jehovah were fashioned—even then, "in the beginning was the Word," and in the beginning God's people were one with the Word and "in the beginning He chose them into eternal life."

Our election, then, is eternal. I will not stop to prove it, I only just run over these thoughts for the benefit of young beginners that they may understand what we mean by eternal, absolute election.

IV. And, next, the election is PERSONAL. Here again, our opponents have tried to overthrow election by telling us that it is an election of nations—and not of people. But here the Apostle says, "God has from the beginning chosen you." It is the most miserable shift on earth to make out that God has not chosen persons but nations, because the very same objection that lies against the choice of persons lies against the choice of a nation. If it were not just to choose a person it would be far more unjust to choose a nation, since nations are but the union of multitudes of persons. To choose a nation seems to be a more gigantic crime—if election is a crime—than to choose one person.

Surely to choose ten thousand would be reckoned to be worse than choosing one—to distinguish a whole nation from the rest of mankind seems to be a greater extravaganza in the acts of Divine Sovereignty than the election of one poor mortal and leaving out another. But what are nations but men? What are whole peoples but combinations of different units? A nation is made up of that individual, and that, and that. And if you tell me that God chose the Jews, I say then, He chose that Jew and that Jew and that Jew. And if you say He chooses Britain, then I say He chooses that British man and that British man and that British man.

So that it is the same thing after all. Election then is personal—it must be so. Everyone who reads this text and others like it, will see that Scripture continually speaks of God's people one by one and speaks of them as having been the special subjects of election—

"Sons we are through God's election,
Who in Jesus Christ believe;
By eternal destination
Sovereign Grace we here receive."

We know it is personal election.

V. The other thought is—for my time flies too swiftly to enable me to dwell at length upon these points—that election produces GOOD RESULTS. "He has from the beginning chosen you unto sanctification of the Spirit and belief of the Truth." How many men mistake the doctrine of election altogether! And how my soul burns and boils at the recollection of the terrible evils that have accrued from the spoiling and the wresting of that glorious portion of God's glorious Truth!

How many are there who have said to themselves, "I am elect," and have sat down in sloth and worse than that! They have said, "I am the elect of God," and with both hands they have done wickedness. They have swiftly run to every unclean thing because they have said, "I am the chosen child of God, irrespective of my works, therefore I may live as I like and do what I like." O, Beloved! Let me solemnly warn everyone of you not to carry the truth too far—or, rather not to turn the truth into error, for we cannot carry it too far. We may overstep the truth—we can make that which was meant to be sweet for our comfort a terrible mixture for our destruction.

I tell you there have been thousands of men who have been ruined by misunderstanding election—who have said, "God has elected me to Heaven and to eternal life"—but they have forgotten that it is written, God has elected them "through sanctification of the Spirit and belief of the Truth." This is God's election—election to sanctification and to faith. God chooses His people to be holy and to be Believers. How many of you here, then, are Believers? How many of my congregation can put their hands upon their hearts and say, "I trust in God that I am sanctified"? Is there one of you who says, "I am elect"?

One of you says, "I trust I am elect"—but I jog your memory about some vicious act that you committed during the last six days. Another of you says, "I am elect"—but I would look you in the face and say, "Elect? You are a most cursed hypocrite and that is all you are." Others would say, "I am elect"—but I would remind them that they neglect the mercy seat and do not pray. Oh, Beloved! Never think you are elect unless you are holy. You may come to Christ as a sinner but you may not come to Christ as an elect person until you can see your holiness. Do not misconstrue what I say—do not say, "I am elect," and yet think you can be living in sin.

That is impossible. The elect of God are holy. They are not pure, they are not perfect, they are not spotless—but taking their life as a whole they are holy persons. They are marked and distinct from others—and no man has a right to conclude himself elect except in his holiness. He may be elect and yet lying in darkness but he has no right to believe it. No one can say it, if there is no evidence of it. The man may live one day but he is dead at present. If you are walking in the fear of God, trying to please Him and to obey His Commandments, doubt not that your name has been written in the Lamb's Book of Life from before the foundation of the world.

And, lest this should be too high for you, note the other mark of election, which is faith—belief of the Truth of God. Whoever believes God's Truth and believes on Jesus Christ is elect. I frequently meet with poor souls who are fretting and worrying themselves about this thought—"What if I should not be elect!" "Oh, Sir," they say, "I know I put my trust in Jesus. I know I believe in His name and trust in His blood. But what if I should not be elect?" Poor dear creature! You do not know much about the Gospel or you would never talk so, for he that believes is elect. Those who are elect, are elect unto sanctification and unto faith. If you have faith you are one of God's elect. You may know it and ought to know it for it is an absolute certainty.

If you, as a sinner, look to Jesus Christ this morning and say—

"Nothing in my hands I bring,
Simply to Your Cross I cling,"

then you are elect. I am not afraid of election frightening poor saints or sinners. There are many divines who tell the enquirer, "election has nothing to do with you." That is very bad, because the poor soul is not to be silenced like that. If you could silence him so it might be well—but he will think of it, he can't help it. Say to him then, if you believe on the Lord Jesus Christ you are elect. If you will cast yourself on Jesus, you are elect. I tell you—the chief of sinners—this morning—I tell you in His name—if you will come to God without any works of your own, cast yourself on the blood and righteousness of Jesus Christ—if you will come now and trust in Him, you are elect—you were loved of God from before the foundation of the world, for you could not do that unless God had given you the power and had chosen you to do it.

Now you are safe and secure if you do but come and cast yourself on Jesus Christ and wish to be saved and to be loved by Him. But think not that any man will be saved without faith and without holiness. Do not conceive, my Hearers, that some decree, passed in the dark ages of eternity will save your souls, unless you believe in Christ. Do not sit down and fancy that you are to be saved without faith and holiness. That is a most abominable and accursed heresy and has ruined thousands.

Lay not election as a pillow for you to sleep on, or you may be ruined. God forbid that I should be sewing pillows under armholes that you may rest comfortably in your sins. Sinner! There is nothing in the Bible to palliate your sins. But if you are condemned, O Man! If you are lost, O Woman! You will not find in this Bible one drop to cool your tongue, or one doctrine to palliate your guilt. Your damnation will be entirely your own fault and your sin will richly merit it—because you believe not you are condemned. "You believe not because you are not of My sheep. You will not come to Me that you might have life."

Do not fancy that election excuses sin—do not dream of it—do not rock yourself in sweet complacency in the thought of your irresponsibility. You are responsible. We must give you both things. We must have Divine Sovereignty and we must have man's responsibility. We must have election, but we must ply your hearts—we must send God's Truth at you. We must speak to you and remind you of this, that while it is written, "In Me is your help," yet it is also written, "O Israel, you have destroyed yourself."

VI. Now, lastly, what are the true and legitimate tendencies of right conceptions concerning the doctrine of election? First, I will tell you what the doctrine of election will make saints do under the blessing of God. And, secondly what it will do for sinners if God blesses it to them.

First, I think election, to a saint, is one of the most stripping doctrines in all the world—to take away all trust in the flesh or all reliance upon anything except Jesus Christ. How often do we wrap ourselves up in our own righteousness and array ourselves with the false pearls and gems of our own works and doings? We begin to say, "Now I shall be saved, because I have this and that evidence." Instead of that, it is naked faith that saves—that faith and that alone unites to the Lamb irrespective of works, although it is productive of them.

How often do we lean on some work other than that of our own Beloved Jesus and trust in some might, other than that which comes from on High? Now if we would have this might taken from us we must consider election. Pause, my Soul, and consider this. God loved you before you had a being. He loved you when you were dead in trespasses and sins and sent His Son to die for you. He purchased you with His precious blood before you could say His name. Can you then be proud?

I know nothing, nothing again, that is more humbling for us than this doctrine of election. I have sometimes fallen prostrate before it when endeavoring to understand it. I have stretched my wings and, eagle-like, I have soared towards the sun. Steady has been my eye and true my wing for a season. But, when I came near it and the one thought possessed me—"God has from the beginning chosen you unto salvation," I was lost in its lustre. I was staggered with the mighty thought—and from the dizzy elevation down came my soul, prostrate and broken, saying, "Lord, I am nothing, I am less than nothing. Why me? Why me?"

Friends, if you want to be humbled, study election, for it will make you humble under the influence of God's Spirit. He who is proud of his election is not elect—and he who is humbled under a sense of it may believe that he is. He has every reason to believe that he is, for it is one of the most blessed effects of election that it helps us to humble ourselves before God.

Once again—Election in the Christian should make him very fearless and very bold. No man will be so bold as he who believes that he is elect of God. What cares he for man if he is chosen of his Maker? What will he care for the pitiful chirpings of some tiny sparrows when he knows that he is an eagle of a royal race? Will he care when the beggar points at him—when the blood royal of heaven runs in his veins? Will he fear if all the world stand against him? If earth be all in arms abroad, he dwells in perfect peace—for he is in the secret place of the tabernacle of the Most High, in the great pavilion of the Almighty.

"I am God's," he says, "I am distinct from other men. They are of an inferior race. Am I not noble? Am I not one of the aristocrats of Heaven? Is not my name written in God's Book?" Does he care for the world? No—like the lion that cares not for the barking of the dog, he smiles at all his enemies—and when they come too near him, he moves himself and dashes them to pieces. What cares he for them? He walks about them like a colossus—while little men walk under him and understand him not.

His brow is made of iron, his heart is of flint—what does he care for man? No—if one universal hiss came up from the wide world, he would smile at it, for he would say—

"He that has made his refuge God,
Shall find a most secure abode."

I am one of His elect. I am chosen of God and precious—and though the world cast me out, I fear not. Ah, you time-serving professors, some of you will bend like the willows. There are few oaken-Christians nowadays that can stand the storm—and I will tell you the reason. It is because you do not believe yourselves to be elect. The man who knows he is elect will be too proud to sin—he will not humble himself to commit the acts of common people.

The believer in God's Truth will say, "I compromise my principles? I change my doctrines? I lay aside my views? I hide what I believe to be true? No! Since I know I am one of God's elect, in the very teeth of all men I shall speak God's Truth, whatever man may say." Nothing makes a man so truly bold as to feel that he is God's elect. He shall not quiver, he shall not shake—who knows that God has chosen him.

Moreover, election will make us holy. Nothing under the gracious influence of the Holy Spirit can make a Christian more holy than the thought that he is chosen. "Shall I sin," he says, "after God has chosen me? Shall I transgress after such love? Shall I go astray after so much loving kindness and tender mercy? No, my God, since You have chosen me, I will love You. I will live to You—

"Since You, the everlasting God,
My Father are become."

I will give myself to You to be Yours forever, by election and by redemption, casting myself on You and solemnly consecrating myself to Your service.

And now, lastly, to the ungodly. What says election to you? First, you ungodly ones, I will excuse you for a moment. There are many of you who do not like election and I cannot blame you for it, for I have heard those preach election who have sat down and said, "I have not one word to say to the sinner." Now, I say you ought to dislike such preaching as that and I do not blame you for it. But, I say, take courage, take hope, O you Sinner, that there is election!

So far from dispiriting and discouraging you, it is a very hopeful and joyous thing that there is an election. What if I told you perhaps none can be saved, none are ordained to eternal life? Would you not tremble and fold your hands in hopelessness and say, "Then how can I be saved, since none are elect?" But, I say, there is a multitude of elect, beyond all counting—a host that no mortal can number. Therefore, take heart, poor Sinner! Cast away your despondency—may you not be elect as well as any other?—for there is a host innumerable chosen! There is joy and comfort for you!

Then, not only take heart, but go and try the Master. Remember, if you were not elect, you would lose nothing by it. What did the four lepers say? "Let us fall unto the host of the Syrians, for if we stay here we must die and if we go to them we can but die." O Sinner! Come to the Throne of electing mercy! You may die where you are. Go to God—and, even supposing He should spurn you, suppose His uplifted hand should drive you away—a thing impossible—yet you will not lose anything. You will not be more damned for that. Besides, supposing you are damned, you would have the satisfaction at least of being able to lift up your eyes in Hell and say, "God, I asked mercy of You and You would not grant it. I sought it, but You did refuse it."

That you shall never say, O Sinner! If you go to Him and ask Him, you shall receive—for He never has spurned one yet! Is not that hope for you? What though there is an allotted number, yet it is true that all who seek belong to that number. Go and seek—and if you should be the first one to go to Hell, tell the devils that you did perish thus—tell the demons that you are a castaway after having come as a guilty sinner to Jesus. I tell you it would disgrace the Eternal—with reverence to His name—and He would not allow such a thing. He is jealous of His honor and He could not allow a sinner to say that.

But ah, poor Soul! Do not think thus, that you can lose anything by coming. There is yet one more thought—do you love the thought of election this morning? Are you willing to admit its justice? Do you say, "I feel that I am lost. I deserve it and if my brother is saved I cannot murmur. If God destroys me, I deserve it, but if He saves the person sitting beside me, He has a right to do what He will with His own and I have lost nothing by it."

Can you say that honestly from your heart? If so, then the doctrine of election has had its right effect on your spirit and you are not far from the kingdom of Heaven. You are brought where you ought to be, where the Spirit wants you to be—and being so this morning, depart in peace! God has forgiven your sins. You would not feel that if you were not pardoned—you would not feel that if the Spirit of God were not working in you. Rejoice, then, in this! Let your hope rest on the Cross of Christ. Think not on election, but on Christ Jesus. Rest on Jesus—Jesus first, last and without end.

LIMITED ATONEMENT

Sermon No. 181
Delivered on February 28th, 1858
by Rev. C. H. Spurgeon
at The Music Hall
Royal Surrey Gardens

LIMITED ATONEMENT

(PARTICULAR REDEMPTION)

"Even as the Son of Man came not to be ministered unto, but to minister, And to give His life a ransom for many."

—Matthew 20:28

WHEN first it was my duty to occupy this pulpit and preach in this hall, my congregation assumed the appearance of an irregular mass of persons collected from all the streets of this city to listen to the Word. I was then simply an Evangelist, preaching to many who had not heard the Gospel before. By the Grace of God, the most blessed change has taken place and now, instead of having an irregular multitude gathered together, my congregation is as fixed as that of any minister in the whole city of London! I can from this pulpit observe the countenances of my friends who have occupied the same places, as nearly as possible, for these many months. And I have the privilege and the pleasure of knowing that a very large proportion, certainly three-fourths of the persons who meet together here are not persons who stray here from curiosity, but are my regular and constant hearers. And observe that my character has also been changed! From being an Evangelist, it is now my business to become your pastor. You were once a motley group assembled to listen to me but now we are bound together by the ties of love. Through association we have grown to love and respect each other and now you have become the sheep of my pasture and members of my flock. And I have now the privilege of assuming the position of a pastor in this place, as well as in the Chapel where I labor in the evening. I think, then, it will strike the judgment of every person that as both the congregation and the office have now changed, the teaching itself should in some measure suffer a difference.

It has been my desire to address you from the simple Truths of the Gospel. I have very seldom, in this place, attempted to dive into the deep things of God. A text which I have thought suitable for my congregation in the evening, I should not have made the subject of discussion in this place in the morning. There are many high and mysterious Doctrines which I have often taken the opportunity of handling in my own place that I have not taken the liberty of introducing here, regarding you as a company of people casually gathered together to hear the Word. But now, since the circumstances are changed, the teaching will also be changed. I shall not now simply confine myself to the Doctrine of the faith, or the teaching of Believer's Baptism. I shall not stay upon the surface of matters, but shall venture, as God shall guide me, to enter into those things that lie at the basis of the religion that we hold so dear. I shall not blush to preach before you the Doctrine of God's

Divine Sovereignty. I shall not stagger to preach in the most unreserved and unguarded manner the Doctrine of Election. I shall not be afraid to propound the great Truth of the Final Perseverance of the Saints. I shall not withhold that undoubted Truth of Scripture—the Effectual Calling of God's Elect. I shall endeavor, as God shall help me, to keep back nothing from you who have become my flock. Seeing that many of you have now "tasted that the Lord is gracious," we will endeavor to go through the whole system of the Doctrines of Grace—that saints may be edified and built up in their most holy faith!

I begin this morning with the Doctrine of Redemption. "He gave His life a ransom for many." The Doctrine of Redemption is one of the most important Doctrines of the system of faith. A mistake on this point will inevitably lead to a mistake through the entire system of our belief!

Now, you are aware that there are different theories of Redemption. All Christians hold that Christ died to redeem, but all Christians do not teach the same Redemption! We differ as to the nature of Atonement and as to the design of Redemption. For instance, the Arminian holds that Christ, when He died, did not die with an intent to save any particular person. And they teach that Christ's death does not, in itself, secure beyond doubt the salvation of any man living. They believe that Christ died to make the salvation of all men possible, or that by the doing of something else, any man who pleases may attain unto eternal life! Consequently, they are obliged to hold that if man's will would not give way and voluntarily surrender to Divine Grace, then Christ's Atonement would be worthless! They hold that there was no particularity and specialty in the death of Christ. Christ died, according to them, as much for Judas in Hell as for Peter who mounted to Heaven! They believe that for those who are consigned to eternal fire, there was as true and real a Redemption made as for those who now stand before the Throne of the Most High! Now we believe no such thing! We hold that Christ, when He died, had an objective in view and that objective will most assuredly and beyond a doubt, be accomplished! We measure the design of Christ's death by the effect of it. If anyone asks us, "What did Christ design to do by His death?" We answer that question by asking him another—"What has Christ done, or what will Christ do by His death?" We declare that the measure of the effect of Christ's love is the measure of the design of it! We cannot so belie our reason as to think that the intention of Almighty God could be frustrated or that the design of so great a thing as the Atonement can by any way whatever, be missed of. We hold—we are not afraid to say what we believe—that Christ came into this world with the intention of saving "a multitude which no man can number." And we believe that as the result of this, every person for whom He died must, beyond the shadow of a doubt, be cleansed from sin and stand, washed in His blood, before the Father's Throne. We do not believe that Christ made any effectual Atonement for those who are forever damned! We dare not think that His blood was ever shed with the intention of saving those whom God foreknew would never be saved—and some of whom were even in Hell when Christ, according to some men's account, died to save them!

I have thus just stated our theory of Redemption and hinted at the differences which exist between two great parties in the professing Church. It shall be now my endeavor to show the greatness of the Redemption of Christ Jesus. And by so doing I hope to be enabled by God's Spirit to bring out the whole of the great system of Redemption so that it may be understood by us all, even if all of us cannot receive it. You must bear this in mind that some of you, perhaps, may be ready to dispute things which I assert. But you will remember that this is nothing to me. I shall at all times teach those things which I hold to be true, without let or hindrance from any man breathing! You have the like liberty to do the same in your own places and to preach your own views in your own assemblies, as I claim the right to preach mine, fully, and without hesitation!

Christ Jesus "gave His life a ransom for many." And by that ransom He worked out for us a great Redemption. I shall endeavor to show the greatness of this Redemption, measuring it in five ways. We shall note its greatness, first of all, from the heinousness of our own guilt, from which He has delivered us. Secondly, we shall measure His Redemption by the sternness of Divine Justice. Thirdly, we shall measure it by the price which He paid—the pangs which He endured. Then we shall endeavor to magnify it by noting the deliverance which He actually worked out. And we shall close by noticing the vast number for whom this Redemption is made, who in our text are described as "many."

I. First, then, we shall see that the Redemption of Christ was no little thing, if we do but measure it, first, by our OWN SINS. My Brothers and Sisters, for a moment look at the hole of the pit from where you were dug—and the quarry where you were hewn. You who have been washed, cleansed and sanctified, pause for a moment and look back at the former state of your ignorance. Think of the sins in which you indulged, the crimes into which you were hurried, the continual rebellion against God in which it was your habit to live. One sin can ruin a soul forever. It is not in the power of the human mind to grasp the infinity of evil that slumbers in the heart of one solitary sin! There is a very infinity of guilt couched in one transgression against the majesty of Heaven. If, then, you and I had sinned but once, nothing but an Atonement infinite in value could ever have washed away the sin and made satisfaction for it! But has it been once that you and I have transgressed? No, my Brothers and Sisters—our iniquities are more in number than the hairs of our head! They have mightily prevailed against us! We might as well attempt to number the sands upon the seashore—or count the drops which in their aggregate make the ocean—as attempt to count the transgressions which have marked our lives! Let us go back to our childhood. How early we began to sin! How we disobeyed our parents and even then learned to make our mouth the house of lies! In our childhood how full of wantonness and waywardness we were! Headstrong and giddy, we preferred our own way and burst through all restraints which godly parents put upon us. Nor did our youth sober us. Wildly we dashed, many of us, into the very midst of the dance of sin! We became leaders in iniquity. We not only sinned, but we taught others to sin. And as for your manhood, you that have entered upon the prime of life—you may be more outwardly sober, you may be somewhat free from the dissipation of your youth—but how little has the man become bettered! Unless the Sovereign Grace of God has renewed us, we are now no better than we were when we began. And even if it has operated, we still have sins to repent of, for we all lay our mouths in the dust and cast ashes on our head and cry, "Unclean! Unclean!

And oh, you that lean wearily on your staffs, the support of your old age—have you not sins still clinging to your garments? Are your lives as white as the snowy hairs that crown your heads? Do you not still feel that transgression besmears the skirts of your robe and mars its spotlessness? How often are you now plunged into the ditch till your own clothes abhor you! Cast your eyes over the sixty, the seventy, the 80 years during which God has spared your lives—can you for a moment think it possible that you can number up your innumerable transgressions, or compute the weight of the crimes which you have committed? O you stars of Heaven! The astronomer may measure your distance and tell your height, but O you sins of mankind, you surpass all thought! O you lofty mountains! The home of the tempest, the birthplace of the storm! Man may climb your summits and stand wonderingly upon your snows—but you hills of sin—you tower higher than our thoughts! You chasms of transgressions—you are deeper than our imagination dares to dive. Do you accuse me of slandering human nature? It is because you know it not! If God had once manifested your heart to yourself, you would bear me witness that so far from exaggerating, my poor words fail to describe the desperateness of our evil! Oh, if we could, each of us, look into our hearts today—if our eyes could be turned within so as to see the iniquity that is engraved as with the point of the diamond upon our stony hearts—we would then say to the minister that however he may depict the desperateness of guilt, yet can he not by any means surpass it! How great then, Beloved, must be the ransom of Christ when He saved us from all these sins? The men for whom Jesus died, however great their sin, when they believe, are sanctified from all their transgressions! Though they may have indulged in every vice and every lust which Satan could suggest—and which human nature could perform—yet once believing, by God's Grace—all their guilt is washed away! Year after year may have coated them with blackness till their sin has become of double dye, but in one moment of faith, one triumphant moment of confidence in Christ—the great Redemption takes away the guilt of numerous years! No, more! If it were possible for all the sins that men have done in thought, or word, or deed since worlds were made, or time began—to meet on one poor head—the great Redemption is all-sufficient to take all these sins away and wash the sinner whiter than the driven snow!

Oh, who shall measure the heights of the Savior's All-Sufficiency? First, tell how high is sin and then remember that as Noah's flood prevailed over the tops of earth's mountains, so the flood of Christ's Redemption prevails over the tops of the mountains of our sins! In Heaven's courts there are today men who once were murderers, thieves, drunkards, whoremongers, blasphemers and persecutors! But they have been washed—they have been sanctified! Ask them from where the brightness of their robes has come and where their purity has been achieved and they, with united breath, will tell you that they have washed their robes and made them white in the blood of the Lamb! O you troubled consciences! O you weary and heavy-laden ones! O you who are groaning on account of sin! The great Redemption now proclaimed to you is all-sufficient for your needs! And though your numerous sins exceed the stars that deck the sky, here is an Atonement made for them all—a river which can overflow the whole of them and carry them away from you forever!

This, then, is the first measure of the Atonement—the greatness of our guilt.

II. Now, secondly, we must measure the great Redemption BY THE STERNNESS OF DIVINE JUSTICE. "God is Love," always loving, but my next proposition does not at all interfere with this assertion—God is sternly just, inflexibly severe in His dealings with mankind! The God of the Bible is not the God of some men's imagination who thinks so little of sin that He passes it by without demanding any punishment for it. He is not the God of the men who imagine that our transgressions are such little things, such mere peccadilloes that the God of Heaven winks at them and suffers them to die forgotten! No. Jehovah, Israel's God has declared concerning Himself, "The Lord your God is a jealous God." It is His own declaration, "I will by no means clear the guilty." "The soul that sins, it shall die." Learn, my Friends, to look upon God as being as severe in His Justice as if He were not loving—and yet as loving as if He were not severe! His love does not diminish His Justice nor does His Justice, in the least degree, make warfare upon His love. The two things are sweetly linked together in the Atonement of Christ. But, mark, we can never understand the fullness of the Atonement till we have first grasped the Scriptural Truth of God's immense Justice. There was never an ill word spoken, nor an ill thought conceived, nor an evil deed done for which God will not have punishment from someone or another. He will either have satisfaction from you, or else from Christ! If you have no Atonement to bring through Christ, you must forever lie paying the debt which you never can pay, in eternal misery—for as surely as God is God—He will sooner lose His Godhead than suffer one sin to go unpunished, or one particle of rebellion not revenged! You may say that this Character of God is cold, stern, and severe. I cannot help what you say of it. It is nevertheless true. Such is the God of the Bible! And though we repeat it is true that He is Love, it is no more true that He is Love than that He is full of Justice—for every good thing meets in God and is carried to perfection—while Love reaches to consummate loveliness, Justice reaches to the sternness of inflexibility in Him. He has no bend, no warp in His Character. No attribute so predominates as to cast a shadow upon the other. Love has its full sway and Justice has no narrower limit than His love. Oh, then, Beloved, think how great must have been the Substitution of Christ when it satisfied God for all the sins of His people! God demands eternal punishment for man's sin. And God has prepared a Hell into which He casts those who die impenitent. Oh, my Brothers and Sisters, can you think what must have been the greatness of the Atonement which was the substitution for all this agony which God would have cast upon us if He had not poured it upon Christ?

Look! Look! Look with solemn eyes through the shades that part us from the world of spirits and see that house of misery which men call Hell! You cannot endure the spectacle! Remember that in that place there are spirits forever paying their debt to Divine Justice, but though some of them have been there these six thousand years sweltering in the flames, they are no nearer a discharge than when they began! And when ten thousand times ten thousand years shall have rolled away, they will no more have made satisfaction to God for their guilt than they have done up till now! And now can you grasp the thought of the greatness of your Savior's Mediation when He paid your debt and paid it all at once so that there now remains not one farthing of debt owing from Christ's people to their God, except a debt of love? To Justice the Believer owes nothing! Though he owed originally so much that eternity would not have been long enough to suffice for the paying of it, yet in one moment Christ paid it all! The man who believes is entirely sanctified from all guilt and set free from all punishment through what Jesus has done! Think, then, how great His Atonement if He has done all this!

I must just pause here and utter another sentence. There are times when God the Holy Spirit shows to men the sternness of Justice in their own consciences. There is a man here today who has just been cut to the heart with a sense of sin. He was once a free man, a libertine, in bondage to none. But now the arrow of the Lord sticks fast in his heart and he has come under a bondage worse than that of Egypt! I see him today—he tells me that his guilt haunts him everywhere. The Negro slave, guided by the pole star, may escape the cruelties of his master and reach another land where he may be free, but this man feels that if he were to wander the whole world over he could not escape from guilt. He that has been bound by many irons can not find a file that can unbind him and set him at liberty! This man tells you that he has tried prayers and tears and good works, but cannot get the shackles from his wrists. He still feels as a lost sinner—and emancipation—do what he may, seems to him impossible! The captive in the dungeon is sometimes free in thought, though not in body. Through his dungeon walls his spirit leaps and flies to the stars, free as the eagle that is no man's slave. But this man is a slave in his thoughts—he cannot think one bright, one happy thought! His soul is cast down within him. The iron has entered into his spirit and he is sorely afflicted. The captive sometimes forgets his slavery in sleep but this man cannot sleep. By night he dreams of Hell; by day he seems to feel it. He bears a burning furnace of flame within his heart and do what he may, he cannot quench it. He has been confirmed, he has been baptized, he takes the sacrament, he attends a Church or he frequents a Chapel. He regards every rubric and obeys every canon—but the fire still burns. He gives his money to the poor; he is ready to give his body to be burned. He feeds the hungry, he visits the sick, he clothes the naked—but the fire still burns—do what he may, he cannot quench it! O, you sons of weariness and woe! This that you feel is God's Justice in full pursuit of you—and happy should you be who feel this—for now to you I preach this glorious Gospel of the blessed God! You are the man for whom Jesus Christ has died! For you He has satisfied stern Justice. And now all you have to do to obtain peace and conscience is just to say to your adversary who pursues you, "Look here! Christ died for me! My good works could not stop you; my tears could not appease you. Look here! There stands the Cross! There hangs the bleeding God! Listen to His death-shriek! Watch Him die! Are you not now satisfied?" And when you have done that, you shall have the peace of God which passes all understanding, which shall keep your heart and mind through Jesus Christ your Lord—and then shall you know the greatness of His Atonement!

III. In the third place, we may measure the greatness of Christ's Redemption by THE PRICE HE PAID. It is impossible for us to know how great were the pangs of our Savior, but yet some glimpse of them will afford us a little idea of the greatness of the price which He paid for us. O Jesus, who shall describe Your agony?—

> **"Come, all you springs,**
> **Dwell in my head and eyes. Come, clouds and rain!**
> **My grief has need of all the watery things,**
> **That Nature has produced. Let every vein**
> **Suck up a river to supply my eyes,**
> **My weary weeping eyes—too dry for me,**
> **Unless they get new conduits, new supplies**
> **To bear them out and with my state agree."**

O Jesus! You were a sufferer from Your birth, a Man of sorrows and grief's acquaintance! Your sufferings tell on You in one perpetual shower until the last dread hour of darkness. Then not in a shower, but in a cloud, a torrent, a cataract of grief Your agonies did dash upon You. See Him yonder! It is a night of frost and cold, but He is all abroad. It is night. He sleeps not—He is in prayer. Listen to His groans! Did ever man wrestle as He wrestles? Go and look in His face! Was ever such suffering depicted upon mortal countenance as you can there behold? Hear His own words? "My soul is exceedingly sorrowful, even unto death." He rises. He is seized by traitors and is dragged away. Let us step to the place where just now He was engaged in agony. O God! And what is this we see? What is this that stains the ground? It is blood! From where did it come? Had He some wound which oozed afresh through His dire struggle? Ah, no. "He sweat, as it were, great drops of blood, falling down to the ground." O agonies that surpass the word by which we name you! O sufferings that cannot be compassed in language! What could you be that thus could work upon the Savior's blessed frame and force a bloody sweat to fall from His entire body?

This is the beginning—this is the opening of the tragedy. Follow Him mournfully, you sorrowing Church, to witness the consummation of it. He is hurried through the streets. He is first to one bar and then to another. He is cast and condemned before the Sanhedrin. He is mocked by Herod, He is tried by Pilate. His sentence is pronounced—"Let Him be crucified!" And now the tragedy comes to its height. His back is bared. He is tied to the low Roman column. The bloody scourge plows furrows on His back. And with one stream of blood His back is red—a crimson robe that proclaims Him emperor of misery! He is taken into the guard room. His eyes are bound and then they buffet Him and say, "Prophesy, who it was that smote You?" They spit into His face. They plait a crown of thorns and press His temples with it. They array Him in a purple robe. They bow their knees and mock Him. All silently He stands. He answers not a word. "When He was reviled, He reviled not again," but committed Himself unto Him whom He came to serve. And now they take Him and with many a jeer and jibe they drive Him from the place and hurry Him through the streets. Emaciated by continual fasting and depressed with agony of spirit, He stumbles beneath His Cross." Daughters of Jerusalem! He faints in your streets! They raise Him up. They put His Cross upon another's shoulders and they urge Him on, perhaps with many a spear-prick, till at last He reaches the mount of doom. Rough soldiers seize Him and hurl Him on His back. The transverse wood is laid beneath Him, His arms are stretched to reach the necessary distance. The nails are grasped. Four hammers at one moment drive four nails through the most tender parts of His body! And there He lies upon His own place of execution, dying on His Cross. It is not done yet. The Cross is lifted by the rough soldiers. There is the socket prepared for it. It is dashed into its place. They fill up the place with earth. And there it stands.

But look at the Savior's limbs, how they quiver! Every bone has been put out of joint by the dashing of the Cross into that socket! How He weeps! How He sighs! How He sobs! No, more—listen how at last He shrieks in agony, "My God, My God, why have You forsaken Me?" O sun, no wonder you did shut your eyes and look no longer upon a deed so cruel! O rocks! No wonder that you did melt and rend your hearts with sympathy when your Creator died! Never man suffered as this Man suffered! Even death itself relented and many of those who had been in their graves arose and came into the city. This, however, is but the outward. Believe me, Brothers and Sisters, the inward was far worse. What our Savior suffered in His body was nothing compared to what He endured in His soul! You cannot guess and I cannot help you to guess what He endured within. Suppose for one moment—to repeat a sentence I have often used—suppose a man who has passed into Hell—suppose his eternal torment could all be brought into one hour? And then suppose it could be multiplied by the number of the saved, which is a number past all human enumeration—can you now think what a vast aggregate of misery there would have been in the sufferings of all God's people if they had been punished through all eternity?

And remember that Christ had to suffer an equivalent for all the Hells of all His redeemed! I can never express that thought better than by using those oft-repeated words—it seemed as if Hell was put into His cup—He seized it and, "At one tremendous draught of love, He drank damnation dry." So that there was nothing left of all the pangs and miseries of Hell for His people to ever endure! I say not that He suffered the same, but He did endure an equivalent for all this and gave God the satisfaction for all the sins of all His people—and consequently gave Him an equivalent for all their punishment! Now can you dream, can you guess the great Redemption of our Lord Jesus Christ?

IV. I shall be very brief upon the next head. The fourth way of measuring the Savior's agonies is this—we must compute them by THE GLORIOUS DELIVERANCE WHICH HE HAS EFFECTED.

Rise up, Believer, stand up in your place and this day testify to the greatness of what the Lord has done for you! Let me tell it for you! I will tell your experience and mine in one breath. Once my soul was laden with sin. I had revolted against God and grievously transgressed. The terrors of the Law got hold upon me. The pangs of conviction seized me. I saw myself guilty. I looked to Heaven and I saw an angry God sworn to punish me. I looked beneath me and I saw a yawning Hell ready to devour me! I sought, by good works, to satisfy my conscience. But all in vain! I endeavored, by attending to the ceremonies of religion, to appease the pangs that I felt within—but all without effect. My soul was exceedingly sorrowful almost unto death. I could have said with the ancient mourner, "My soul chooses strangling and death rather than life." This was the great question that always perplexed me—"I have sinned. God must punish me. How can He be just if He does not? Then, since He is just, what is to become of me?" At last my eyes turned to that sweet Word which says, "The blood of Jesus Christ His Son cleans from all sin." I took that text to my chamber. I sat there and meditated. I saw one hanging on a Cross. It was my Lord Jesus. There was the crown of thorns and there the emblems of unequalled and peerless misery. I looked upon Him and my thoughts recalled that Word which says, "This is a faithful saying, and worthy of all acceptation, that Christ Jesus came into the world to save sinners." Then said I within myself, "Did this Man die for sinners? I am a sinner. Then He died for me! Those He died for He will save. He died for sinners. I am a sinner. He died for me! He will save me." My soul relied upon that Truth. I looked to Him—and as I "viewed the flowing of His soul-redeeming blood," my spirit rejoiced, for I could say—

> **"Nothing in my hands I bring,**
> **Simply to His Cross I cling!**
> **Naked I look to Him for dress,**
> **Helpless, I come to Him for Grace!**
> **Black, I to this fountain fly—**
> **Wash me, Savior, or I die!"**

And now, Believer, you shall tell the rest. The moment that you believed, your burden rolled from your shoulder and you became light as air. Instead of darkness you had light! For the garments of heaviness, you had the robes of praise. Who shall tell of your joy since then? You have sung on earth hymns of Heaven and in your peaceful soul you have anticipated the eternal Sabbath of the redeemed. Because you have believed, you have entered into rest. Yes, tell it to the whole world over—they who believe, by Jesus' death are justified from all things from which they could not be freed by the works of the Law! Tell it in Heaven—none can lay anything to the charge of God's elect! Tell it upon earth—God's redeemed are free from sin in Jehovah's sight! Tell it even in Hell—God's Elect can never go there—Christ has died for His Elect and who is he that shall condemn them?

V. I have hurried over that to come to the last point which is the sweetest of all! Jesus Christ, we are told in our text, came into the world, "to give His life a ransom for many." The greatness of Christ's Redemption may be measured by the EXTENT OF THE DESIGN OF IT. He gave His life "a ransom for many." I must now return to that controverted point again. We are often told (I mean those of us who are commonly nicknamed by the title of Calvinists—and we are not very much ashamed of that. We think that Calvin, after all, knew more about the Gospel than almost any uninspired man who has ever lived)! We are often told that we limit the Atonement of Christ because we say that Christ has not made a satisfaction for all men, or all men would be saved. Now, our reply to this is that, on the other hand, our opponents limit it—we do not! The Arminians say

Christ died for all men. Ask them what they mean by it. Did Christ die so as to secure the salvation of all men? They say, "No, certainly not." We ask them the next question—Did Christ die so as to secure the salvation of any man in particular? They answer, "No." They are obliged to admit this if they are consistent. They say "No, Christ has died that any man may be saved if—and then follow certain conditions of salvation. We say, then, we will just go back to the old statement—Christ did not die so as beyond a doubt to secure the salvation of anybody, did He? You must say, "No." You are obliged to say so, for you believe that even after a man has been pardoned, he may yet fall from Grace and perish. Now, who is it that limits the death of Christ? Why, you! You say that Christ did not die so as to Infallibly secure the salvation of anybody. We beg your pardon, when you say we limit Christ's death! We say, "No, my dear Sir, it is you that do it. We say Christ so died that He Infallibly secured the salvation of a multitude that no man can number, who through Christ's death not only may be saved but are saved, must be saved and cannot by any possibility run the hazard of being anything but saved! You are welcome to your atonement. You may keep it. We will never renounce ours for the sake of it."

Now, Beloved, when you hear anyone laughing or jeering at a Limited Atonement, you may tell him this—general Atonement is like a great wide bridge with only half an arch. It does not go across the stream. It only professes to go half way—it does not secure the salvation of anybody. Now, I had rather put my foot upon a bridge as narrow as Hungerford, which went all the way across, than on a bridge that was as wide as the world, if it did not go all the way across the stream! I am told it is my duty to say that all men have been redeemed and I am told that there is a Scriptural warrant for it—"Who gave Himself a ransom for all, to be testified in due time." Now, that looks like a very great argument, indeed, on the other side of the question! For instance, look here—"The whole world is gone after Him." Did all the world go after Christ?

"Then went all Judea and were baptized of Him in Jordan." Was all Judea, or all Jerusalem baptized in Jordan? "You are of God, little children," and "the whole world lies in the Wicked One." Does "the whole world" there mean everybody? If so, how was it, then, that there were some who were "of God"? The words, "world," and, "all," are used in some seven or eight senses in Scripture. And it is very rarely that, "all," means all persons taken individually! The words are generally used to signify that Christ has redeemed some of all sorts—some Jews, some Gentiles, some rich, some poor—and has not restricted His Redemption to either Jew or Gentile.

Leaving controversy, however, I will now answer a question. Tell me then, Sir, who did Christ die for? Will you answer me a question or two and I will tell you whether He died for you. Do you need a Savior? Do you feel that you need a Savior? Are you this morning conscious of sin? Has the Holy Spirit taught you that you are lost? Then Christ died for you and you will be saved! Are you this morning conscious that you have no hope in the world but Christ? Do you feel that you, of yourself, cannot offer an Atonement that can satisfy

God's Justice? Have you given up all confidence in yourselves? And can you say upon your bended knees, "Lord, save, or I perish"? Christ died for you!

If you are saying this morning, "I am as good as I ought to be. I can get to Heaven by my own good works," then, remember, the Scripture says of Jesus, "I came not to call the righteous, but sinners to repentance." So long as you are in that state I have no Atonement to preach to you! But if this morning you feel guilty, wretched, conscious of your guilt and are ready to take Christ to be your only Savior, I can not only say to you that you may be saved, but what is better still, that you will be saved! When you are stripped of everything but hope in Christ. When you are prepared to come empty handed and take Christ to be your All and to be yourself nothing at all—then you may look up to Christ and you may say, "You dear, You bleeding Lamb of God! Your griefs were endured for me. By Your stripes I am healed and by Your sufferings I am pardoned." And then see what peace of mind you will have—for if Christ has died for you, you cannot be lost! God will not punish twice for one thing.

If God punished Christ for your sin, He will never punish you. "Payment, God's Justice cannot twice demand first, at the bleeding Surety's hand, and then again at mine." We can today, if we believe in Christ, march to the very Throne of God, stand there, and if it is said, "Are you guilty?" We can say, "Yes, guilty." But if the question is put, "What have you to say why you should not be punished for your guilt?" We can answer, "Great God, Your Justice and Your Love are both our guarantees that You will not punish us for sin. For did You not punish Christ for sin for us? How can You, then, be Just—how can You be God at all, if You punish Christ the Substitute, and then punish man himself afterwards?"

Your only question is, "Did Christ die for me?" And the only answer we can give is—"This is a faithful saying, and worthy of all acceptation, that Christ came into the world to save sinners." Can you write your name down among the sinners? Not among the complimentary sinners, but among those that feel it, bemoan it, lament it, seek mercy on account of it? Are you a sinner? That felt, that known, that professed—you are now invited to believe that Jesus Christ died for you because you are a sinner—and you are bid to cast yourself upon this great immovable Rock and find eternal security in the Lord Jesus Christ!

Sermon No. 73
Delivered on April 6th, 1856
by Rev. C. H. Spurgeon
at New Park Street Chapel, Southwark

IRRESISTABLE GRACE

(EFFECTUAL CALLING)

"When Jesus came to the place,
He looked up and saw him and
said unto him, Zaccheus, make
haste and come down; for today
must I abide at your house."

—Luke 19:5

Notwithstanding our firm belief that you are, for the most part, well instructed in the doctrines of the everlasting Gospel, we are continually reminded in our conversation with young converts how absolutely necessary it is to repeat our former lessons and repeatedly assert and prove over and over again those doctrines which lie at the basis of our holy religion. Our friends, therefore, who have many years ago been taught the great doctrine of effectual calling, will believe that while I preach very simply this morning, the sermon is intended for those who are young in the fear of the Lord, that they may better understand this great starting point of God in the heart, the effectual calling of men by the Holy Spirit.

I shall use the case of Zaccheus as a great illustration of the doctrine of effectual calling. You remember the story. Zaccheus had a curiosity to see the wonderful man, Jesus Christ, who was turning the world upside down and causing an immense excitement in the minds of men. We sometimes find fault with curiosity and say it is sinful to come to the house of God from that motive. I am not quite sure that we should hazard such an assertion. The motive is not sinful, though certainly it is not virtuous—yet it has often been proved that curiosity is one of the best allies of grace. Zaccheus, moved by this motive, desired to see Christ—but there were two obstacles in the way—first, there was such a crowd of people that he could not get near the Savior. Second, he was so exceedingly short in stature that there was no hope of his reaching over people's heads to catch a glimpse of Him.

What did he do? He did as the boys were doing—for the boys of old times were no doubt just like the boys of the present age—they were perched up in the boughs of the tree to look at Jesus as He passed along. Elderly man though he is, Zaccheus jumps up and there he sits among the children. The boys are too much afraid of that stern old Publican, whom their fathers dreaded, to push him down or cause him any inconvenience. Look at him there. With what anxiety he is peeping down to see which is Christ—for the Savior had no pompous distinction. No one is walking before Him with a silver mace. He did not hold a golden crozier in His hand—He had no pontifical dress. In fact, He was just dressed like those around Him. He had a coat like that of a common peasant, made of one piece from top to bottom. Zaccheus could scarcely distinguish Him. However, before he has caught a sight of Christ, Christ has fixed His eye upon him and standing under the tree, He looks up and says, "Zaccheus, make haste and come down; for today I must abide at your house." Down comes Zaccheus. Christ goes to his house. Zaccheus becomes Christ's follower and enters into the kingdom of Heaven.

1. Now, first, effectual calling is a very gracious Truth of God. You may guess this from the fact that Zaccheus was a character whom we should suppose the last to be saved. He belonged to a bad city—Jericho—a city which had been cursed and no one would suspect that anyone would come out of Jericho to be saved. It was near Jericho that the man fell among thieves—we trust Zaccheus had no hand in it—but there are some who, while they are Publicans, can be thieves, also. We might as well expect converts from St. Giles's, or the lowest parts of London, from the worst and vilest dens of infamy, as from Jericho in those days.

Ah, my Brethren, it matters not where you come from—you may come from one of the dirtiest streets, one of the worst back slums in London—if effectual grace calls you, it is an effectual call, which knows no distinction of place. Zaccheus also was of an exceedingly bad trade and probably cheated the people in order to enrich himself. Indeed, when Christ went into his house, there was an universal murmur that He had gone to be a guest with a man that was a sinner. But, my Brethren, grace knows no distinction. It is no respecter of persons. God calls whom He wills and He called this worst of Publicans, in the worst of cities, from the worst of trades. Besides, Zaccheus was one who was the least likely to be saved because he was rich. It is true, rich and poor are welcome—no one has the least excuse for despair because of his condition—yet it is a fact that "not many great men" after the flesh, "not many mighty" are called, but "God has chosen the poor of this world—rich in faith."

But even here grace knows no distinction. The rich Zaccheus is called from the tree. Down he comes and he is saved. I have thought it one of the greatest instances of God's condescension that He can look down on man. But I will tell you there was a greater condescension than that when Christ looked up to see Zaccheus. For God to look down on His creatures—that is mercy—but for Christ so to humble Himself that He has to look up to one of His own creatures—that becomes mercy, indeed!

Ah, many of you have climbed up the tree of your own good works and perched yourselves in the branches of your holy actions and are trusting in the free will of the poor creature, or resting in some worldly maxim. Nevertheless, Christ looks up even to proud sinners and calls them down. "Come down," says He, "today I must abide at your house." Had Zaccheus been a humble-minded man, sitting by the wayside, or at the feet of Christ, we should then have admired Christ's mercy. But here he is lifted up and Christ looks up to him and bids him come down.

2. Next it was a personal call. There were boys in the tree as well as Zaccheus but there was no mistake about

the person who was called. It was, "Zaccheus, make haste and come down." There are other calls mentioned in Scripture. It is said especially, "Many are called, but few are chosen." Now that is not the effectual call which is intended by the Apostle when he said, "Whom He called, them He also justified." That is a general call which many men, yes, all men reject, unless there comes after it the personal, particular call, which makes us Christians. You will bear me witness that it was a personal call that brought you to the Savior. It was some sermon which led you to feel that you were, no doubt, the person intended.

The text, perhaps, was "You, God, see me." And perhaps the minister laid particular stress on the word "me," so that you thought God's eyes were fixed upon you. And before the sermon was concluded you thought you saw God open the books to condemn you and your heart whispered, "Can any hide himself in secret places that I shall not see him? says the Lord." You might have been perched in the window, or stood packed in the aisle—but you had a solemn conviction that the sermon was preached to you and not to other people. God does not call His people in shoals but in units.

"Jesus said unto her, Mary; and she turned and said unto him, Rabboni, which is to say, Master." Jesus sees Peter and John fishing by the lake and He says to them, "Follow Me." He sees Matthew sitting at the table at the receipt of custom and He says unto him, "Arise and follow Me," and Matthew did so. When the Holy Spirit comes home to a man, God's arrow goes into his heart—it does not graze his helmet, or make some little mark upon his armor—it penetrates between the joints of the harness, entering the marrow of the soul. Have you felt, dear Friends, that personal call? Do you remember when a voice said, "Arise, He calls you." Can you look back to when you said, "My Lord, my God"—when you knew the Spirit was striving with you and you said, "Lord, I come to You, for I know that You call me"? I might call the whole of you throughout eternity but if God call one, there will be more effect through His personal call of one than my general call of multitudes.

3. Thirdly, it is a hastening call. "Zaccheus, make haste." The sinner, when he is called by the ordinary ministry, replies, "Tomorrow." He hears a telling sermon and he says, "I will turn to God by-and-by." The tears roll down his cheek but they are wiped away. Some goodness appears but like the cloud of the morning it is dissipated by the sun of temptation. He says, "I solemnly vow from this time to be a reformed man. After I have once more indulged in my darling sin I will renounce my lusts and decide for God." Ah, that is only a minister's call and is good for nothing. Hell, they say, is paved with good intentions. These good intentions are begotten by general calls.

The road to perdition is laid all over with branches of the trees whereon men are sitting, for they often pull down branches from the trees but they do not come down themselves. The straw laid down before a sick man's door causes the wheels to roll more noiselessly. So there are some who strew their path with promises of repentance and so go more easily and noiselessly down to perdition. But God's call is not a call for tomorrow.

"Today if you will hear His voice, harden not your hearts: as in the provocation, when your fathers tempted Me." God's grace always comes with dispatch—and if you are drawn by God, you will run after God and not be talking about delays. Tomorrow—it is not written in the almanac of time.

Tomorrow—it is in Satan's calendar and nowhere else. Tomorrow—it is a rock whitened by the bones of mariners who have been wrecked upon it. Tomorrow is the wrecker's light gleaming on the shore, luring poor ships to destruction. Tomorrow—it is the idiot's cup which he lies at the foot of the rainbow, but which none has ever found. Tomorrow—it is the floating island of Loch Lomond, which none has ever seen. Tomorrow—it is a dream. Tomorrow—it is a delusion. Tomorrow, yes, tomorrow you may lift up your eyes in Hell, being in torment. Yonder clock says "today." Your pulse whispers "today." I hear my heart speak as it beats and it says, "today." Everything cries "today." And the Holy Spirit is in union with these things and says, "Today if you will hear His voice, harden not your hearts." Sinners, are you inclined now to seek the Savior? Are you breathing a prayer now? Are you saying, "Now or never! I must be saved now"? If you are, then I hope it is an effectual call, for Christ, when He gives an effectual call, says, "Zaccheus, make haste."

4. Next, it is a humbling call. "Zaccheus, make haste and come down." Many a time has a minister called men to repentance with a call which has made them proud, exalted them in their own esteem and led them to say, "I can turn to God when I like. I can do so without the

influence of the Holy Spirit." They have been called to go up and not to come down. God always humbles a sinner. Can I not remember when God told me to come down? One of the first steps I had to take was to go right down from my good works. And oh, what a fall was that! Then I stood upon my own self-sufficiency and Christ said, "Come down! I have pulled you down from your good works and now I will pull you down from your self-sufficiency."

Well, I had another fall and I felt sure I had gained the bottom, but Christ said "Come down!" And He made me come down till I fell on some point at which I felt I was not savable. "Down, Sir! come down, yet." And down I came until I had to let go of every branch of the tree of my hopes in despair. Then I said, "I can do nothing. I am ruined." The waters were wrapped round my head and I was shut out from the light of day and thought myself a stranger from the commonwealth of Israel.

"Come down lower yet, Sir! You have too much pride to be saved." Then I was brought down to see my corruption, my wickedness, my filthiness. "Come down," says God, when He means to save. Now, proud Sinners, it is of no use for you to be proud, to stick yourselves up in the trees—Christ will have you down. Oh, you that dwell with the eagle on the craggy rock, you shall come down from your elevation—you shall fall by grace, or you shall fall with a vengeance one day. He "has cast down the mighty from their seat and has exalted the humble and meek."

5. Next, it is an affectionate call. "Today I must abide at your house." You can easily conceive how the faces

of the multitude change! They thought Christ to be the holiest and best of men and were ready to make Him a king. But He says, "Today I must abide at your house." There was one poor Jew who had been inside Zaccheus' house—he had "been on the carpet," as they say in country villages when they are taken before the justice and he recollected what sort of a house it was. He remembered how he was taken in there and his conceptions of it were something like what a fly would have of a spider's den after he had once escaped.

There was another who had been restrained of nearly all his property—the idea he had of walking in there was like walking into a den of lions. "What?" said they, "Is this holy man going into such a den as that, where we poor wretches have been robbed and ill-treated? It was bad enough for Christ to speak to him up in the tree, but the idea of going into his house!" They all murmured at His going to be "a guest with a man who was a sinner." Well, I know what some of His disciples thought—they thought it very imprudent—it might injure His character and He might offend the people. They thought He might have gone to see this man at night, like Nicodemus, and give him an audience when nobody saw Him! To acknowledge such a man publicly was the most imprudent act He could commit.

Why did Christ do as He did? Because He would give Zaccheus an affectionate call. "I will not come and stand at your threshold, or look in at your window, but I will come into your house—the same house where the cries of widows have come into your ears and you have disregarded them. I will come into your parlor, where the weeping of the orphan has never moved your compassion. I will come there, where you, like a ravenous lion have devoured your prey. I will come there, where you have blackened your house and made it infamous. I will come into the place where cries have risen to high Heaven, wrung from the lips of those whom you have oppressed.

"I will come into your house and give you a blessing." Oh, what affection there was in that! Poor Sinner, my Master is a very affectionate Master. He will come into your house. What kind of a house have you got? A house that you have made miserable with your drunkenness—a house you have defiled with your impurity—a house you have defiled with your cursing and swearing—a house where you are carrying on an illegal trade that you would be glad to get rid of? Christ says, "I will come into your house." And I know some houses now that once were dens of sin where Christ comes every morning. Husband and wife, who once only could quarrel and fight, bend their knees together in prayer. Christ comes there at dinnertime, when the workman comes home for his meals. Some of my hearers can scarce come for an hour to their meals but they must have word of prayer and reading of the Scriptures.

Christ comes to them. Where the walls were plastered up with the lascivious songs and idle pictures, there is a Christian almanac in one place. There is a Bible on the chest of drawers—and though it is only one room they live in—if an angel should come in and God should say, "What have you seen in that house?" He would say, "I have seen good furniture, for there is a Bible there—

here and there a religious book—the filthy pictures are pulled down and burned. There are no cards in the man's cupboard now. Christ has come into his house." Oh, what a blessing that we have our household God as well as the Romans! Our God is a household God. He comes to live with His people! He loves the tents of Jacob.

Now, poor rag-muffin Sinner, you who live in the filthiest den in London, if such an one be here, Jesus says to you, "Zaccheus, make haste and come down; for today I must abide at your house."

6. Again, it was not only an affectionate call, but it was an abiding call. Today I must abide at your house." A common call is like this, "Today I shall walk in at your house at one door and out at the other." The common call which is given by the Gospel to all men is a call which operates upon them for a time and then it is all over—but the saving call is an abiding call. When Christ speaks, He does not say, "Make haste, Zaccheus and come down, for I am just coming to look in." No. He says, "I must abide at your house. I am coming to sit down to eat and drink with you. I am coming to have a meal with you. Today I must abide at your house."

"Ah," says one, "you cannot tell how many times I have been impressed, Sir. I have often had a series of solemn convictions and I thought I really was saved—but it all died away—like a dream. When one awakes, all has vanished that he dreamed. So was it with me." Ah, but poor Soul, do not despair. Do you feel the strivings of Almighty Grace within your heart bidding you repent today? If you do, it will be an abiding call. If it is Jesus at work in your soul, He will come and tarry in your heart and consecrate you for His own forever. He says, "I will come and dwell with you and that forever. I will come and say—

> **"Here I will make My settled rest,**
> **No more will go and come;**
> **No more a stranger or a guest,**
> **But Master of this home."**

"Oh," you say, "that is what I want. I want an abiding call, something that will last. I do not want a religion that will wash out, but a fast-color religion." Well, that is the kind of call Christ gives. His ministers cannot give it—but when Christ speaks, He speaks with power and says, "Zaccheus, make haste and come down; for today I must abide at your house."

7. There is one thing, however, I cannot forget and that is that it was a necessary call. Just read it over again. "Zaccheus, make haste and come down; for today I must abide at your house." It was not a thing that He might do, or might not do—it was a necessary call. The salvation of a sinner is as much a matter of necessity with God as the fulfillment of His Covenant that the rain shall no more drown the world. The salvation of every blood-bought child of God is a necessary thing for three reasons:

It is necessary because it is God's purpose. It is necessary because it is Christ's purchase and it is necessary because it is God's promise. It is necessary that the child of God should be saved. Some divines think it is very wrong to lay a stress on the word "must," especially in that passage where it is said, "He must go through Samaria." "Why," they say, "He must needs go through

Samaria because there was no other way He could go and therefore He was forced to go that way." Yes, Gentlemen, we reply, no doubt. But then there might have been another way. Providence made it so that He must go through Samaria and that Samaria should lie in the route He had chosen.

"He must needs go through Samaria." Providence directed man to build Samaria directly in the road and grace constrained the Savior to move in that direction. It was not, "Come down, Zaccheus, because I may abide at your house," but "I must." The Savior felt a strong necessity. Just as much a necessity as there is that man should die. As strong a necessity as there is that the sun should give us light by day and the moon by night—just so much a necessity is there that every blood-bought child of God shall be saved.

"Today I must abide at your house." And oh, when the Lord comes to this—that He must—then He will. What a thing it is with the poor sinner, then, at other times we ask, "Shall I let Him in at all? There is a stranger at the door. He is knocking now—He has knocked before—shall I let Him in?" But this time it is, "I must abide at your house." There was no knocking at the door, but smash went the door into atoms! And in He walked—I must, I shall, I will—I care not for your protecting your vileness, your unbelief. I must, I will—I must abide at your house."

"Ah," says one, "I do not believe God would ever make me to believe as you believe, or become a Christian at all." Ah, but if He shall but say, "Today I must abide at your house," there will be no resistance in you. There are some of you who would scorn the very idea of being a canting Methodist—"What, Sir? Do you suppose I would ever turn into one of your religious people?" No, my Friend, I don't suppose it—I know it for a certainty. If God says "I must," there is no standing against it. Let Him say "must," and it must be.

I will just tell you an anecdote proving this. "A father was about sending his son to college, but as he knew the influence to which he would be exposed, he was not without a deep and anxious solicitude for the spiritual and eternal welfare of his favorite child. Fearing lest the principles of Christian faith, which he had endeavored to instill into his mind would be rudely assailed, but trusting in the efficacy of that Word which is quick and powerful, he purchased, unknown to his son, an elegant copy of the Bible and deposited it at the bottom of his trunk.

The young man entered upon his college career. The restraints of a pious education were soon broken off and he proceeded from speculation to doubts and from doubts to a denial of the reality of religion. After having become in his own estimation, wiser than his father, he discovered one day, while rummaging his trunk, with great surprise and indignation, the sacred deposit. He took it out and while deliberating on the manner in which he should treat it, he determined that he would use it as waste paper, on which to wipe his razor while shaving. Accordingly, every time he went to shave, he tore out a leaf or two of the holy book and thus used it till nearly half the volume was destroyed.

But while he was committing this outrage upon the sacred book, a text now and then met his eye and was carried like a barbed arrow to his heart. At length, he heard a sermon, which discovered to him his own character and his exposure to the wrath of God. It riveted upon his mind the impression which he had received from the last torn leaf of the blessed, yet insulted volume. Had worlds been at his disposal, he would freely have given them all, could they have availed, in enabling him to undo what he had done. At length he found forgiveness at the foot of the Cross. The torn leaves of that sacred volume brought healing to his soul—for they led him to repose on the mercy of God, which is sufficient for the chief of sinners.

I tell you there is not a reprobate walking the streets and defiling the air with his blasphemies. There is not a creature abandoned so as to be well-nigh as bad as Satan himself—if he is a child of life—who is not within the reach of mercy. And if God says, "Today I must abide at your house," He then assuredly will.

Do you feel, my dear Hearer, just now, something, in your mind which seems to say you have held out against the Gospel a long while, but today you can hold out no longer? Do you feel that a strong hand has got hold of you and do you hear a voice saying, "Sinner, I must abide at your house. You have often scorned Me, you have often laughed at Me, you have often spit in the face of mercy, often blasphemed Me, but Sinner, I must abide at your house. You banged the door yesterday in the missionary's face. You burned the tract, you laughed at the minister, you have cursed God's house, you have violated the Sabbath—but, Sinner, I must abide at your house and I will"?

"What? Lord," you say, "abide at my house! Why it is covered all over with iniquity. Abide in my house! Why there is not a chair or a table but would cry out against me. Abide in my house! Why the joists and beams and flooring would all rise up and tell You that I am not worthy to kiss the hem of Your garment. What? Lord, abide at my house!" "Yes," says He, "I must. There is a strong necessity, My powerful love constrains Me and whether you will let Me or not, I am determined to make you willing and you shall let Me in."

Does not this surprise you, poor Trembler—you who thought that mercy's day was gone and that the bell of your destruction had tolled your death-knell? Oh, does not this surprise you, that Christ not only asks you to come to Him, but invites Himself to your table, and what is more, when you would put Him away, kindly says, I must—I will come in"? Only think of Christ going after a sinner, crying after a sinner, begging a sinner to let Him save him—and that is just what Jesus does to His chosen ones.

The sinner runs away from Him, but free grace pursues him and says, "Sinner, come to Christ." And if our hearts are shut up, Christ puts His hand in at the door and if we do not rise, but repulse Him coldly, He says, "I must, I will come in." He weeps over us till His tears win us. He cries after us till His cries prevail—and at last in His own well-determined hour He enters into our heart and there He dwells. "I must abide at your house," said Jesus.

8. And now, lastly, this call was an effectual one, for we see the fruits it brought forth. Open was Zaccheus' door, spread was his table, generous was his heart, washed were his hands, unburdened was his conscience, joyful was his soul. "Here, Lord," says he, "the half of my goods I give to the poor. I dare say I have robbed them of half my property—and now I restore it. And if I have taken anything from anyone by false accusation, I will restore it to him fourfold." Away goes another portion of his property. Ah, Zaccheus, you will go to bed tonight a great deal poorer than when you got up this morning—but infinitely richer, too!

Poor, very poor, in this world's goods, compared with what you were when you first did climb that sycamore tree. But richer—infinitely richer—in heavenly treasure. Sinner, we shall know whether God calls you by this—if He calls, it will be an effectual call—not a call which you hear and then forget—but one which produces good works. If God has called you this morning, down will go that drunken cup, up will go your prayers. If God has called you this morning, there will not be one shutter down today in your shop, but all and you will have a notice stuck up, "This house is closed on the Sabbath and will not again on that day, be opened."

Tomorrow there will be such-and-such worldly amusement—but if God has called you, you will not go. And if you have robbed anybody (and who knows but I may have a thief here), if God calls you, there will be a restoration of what you have stolen—you will give up all that you have—so that you will follow God with all your heart. We do not believe a man to be converted unless he does renounce the error of his ways—unless, practically, he is brought to know that Christ Himself is Master of his conscience and His Law is his delight.

"Zaccheus, make haste and come down, I must abide at your house." And he made haste and came down and Jesus received him joyfully. "And Zaccheus stood and said unto the Lord, Behold, Lord, the half of my goods I give to the poor; and if I have taken anything from any man by false accusation, I restore him fourfold. And Jesus said unto him, This day is salvation come to this house, forasmuch as he also is a son of Abraham. For the Son of Man is come to seek and to save that which was lost."

Now, one or two lessons. A lesson to the proud. Come down, proud heart, come down! Mercy runs in valleys, but it goes not to the mountaintop. Come down, come down, lofty spirit! The lofty city—He lays it low even to the ground and then He builds it up. Again, a lesson to the poor despairing soul—I am glad to see you in God's house this morning—it is a good sign. I care not what you came for. You heard there was a strange kind of man that preached here, perhaps. Never mind about that. You are all quite as strange as he is. It is necessary that there should be strange men to gather in other strange men.

Now, I have a mass of people here. And if I might use a figure, I should compare you to a great heap of ashes, mingled with which are a few steel filings. Now, my sermon, if it is attended with Divine Grace, will be a sort of magnet—it will not attract any of the ashes—they will keep just where they are—but it will draw out the steel filings. I have got a Zaccheus there. There is a Mary up there. A John down there, a Sarah, or a William, or a Thomas there—God's chosen ones—they are steel filings in the congregation of ashes and my Gospel, the Gospel of the blessed God, like a great magnet, draws them out of the heap.

There they come, there they come. Why? Because there was a magnetic power between the Gospel and their hearts. Ah, poor Sinner, come to Jesus, believe His love, trust His mercy. If you have a desire to come, if you are forcing your way through the ashes to get to Christ, then it is because Christ is calling you. Oh, all of you who know yourselves to be sinners—every man, woman and child of you—yes, you little children (for God has given me some of you to be my wages), do you feel yourselves sinners?

Then believe on Jesus and be saved. You have come here from curiosity, many of you. Oh, that you might be met with and saved. I am distressed for you lest you should sink into Hell. Oh, listen to Christ while He speaks to you. Christ says, "Come down." This morning go home and humble yourselves in the sight of God. Go and confess your iniquities that you have sinned against Him. Go home and tell Him that you are a wretch, undone without His sovereign grace.

Then look to Him, for rest assured He has first looked to you. You say, "Sir, oh, I am willing enough to be saved, but I am afraid He is not willing."

Stop! Stop! No more of that! Do you know that is part blasphemy? Not quite all. If you were not ignorant, I would tell you that it was full blasphemy. You cannot look to Christ before He has looked to you. If you are willing to be saved, He gave you that will. Believe on the Lord Jesus Christ and be baptized and you shall be saved. I trust the Holy Spirit is calling you.

Young man up there, young man in the window, make haste! Come down! Old man, sitting in these pews, come down! Merchant in yonder aisle, make haste. Matron and youth, not knowing Christ, oh, may He look at you! Old grandmother, hear the gracious call. And you, young lad, Christ may be looking at you—I trust He is—and saying to you, "Make haste and come down, for today I must abide at your house."

PERSEVERANCE OF THE SAINTS

Sermon No. 75
Delivered on April 20th, 1856
by Rev. C. H. Spurgeon
at New Park Street Chapel, Southwark

PERSEVERANCE OF THE SAINTS
(FINAL PERSEVERANCE)

"For it is impossible for those who were once enlightened and have tasted of the heavenly gift, and were made partakers of the Holy Spirit and have tasted the good word of God, and the powers of the world to come, if they shall fall away, to renew them again unto repentance, seeing they crucify to themselves the Son of God afresh, and put Him to an open shame."

—Hebrews 6:4-6

THERE are some spots in Europe which have been the scenes of frequent warfare, as for instance, the kingdom of Belgium which might be called the battlefield of Europe. War has raged over the whole of Europe, but in some unhappy spots, battle after battle has been fought. So there is scarce a passage of Scripture which has not been disputed between the enemies of the Truth of God and the upholders of it—but this passage with one or two others has been the special subject of attack. This is one of the texts which have been trod under the feet of controversy and there are opinions upon it as adverse as the poles. Some assert that it means one thing and some declare that it means another. We think that some of them approach somewhat near the truth—but others of them desperately err from the mind of the Spirit.

We come to this passage ourselves with the intention to read it with the simplicity of a child and whatever we find therein to state it. And if it may not seem to agree with something we have up to now held, we are prepared to cast away every doctrine of our own rather than one passage of Scripture. Looking at the scope of the whole passage, it appears to us that the Apostle wished to push the disciples on. There is a tendency in the human mind to stop short of the heavenly mark. As soon as ever we have attained to the first principles of religion, have passed through Baptism and understand the resurrection of the dead, there is a tendency in us to sit still—to say, "I have passed from death unto life. Here I may take my stand and rest."

The Christian life was intended not to be a sitting still, but a race, a perpetual motion. The Apostle, therefore, endeavors to urge the disciples forward and make then run with diligence the heavenly race, looking unto Jesus. He tells them that it is not enough to have on a certain day passed through a glorious change—to have experienced at a certain time a wonderful operation of the Spirit. Rather, he teaches them it is absolutely necessary that they should have the Spirit all their lives—that they should, as long as they live, be progressing in the Truth of God. In order to make them persevere, if possible, he shows them that if they do not, they must, most certainly be lost—for there is no other salvation but that which God has already bestowed on them and if that does not keep them—carry them forward and present them spotless before God—there cannot be any other. It is impossible, he says, if you are once enlightened and then fall away, that you should ever be renewed again unto repentance.

We shall, this morning, answer one or two questions. The first question will be, Who are the people here spoken of? Are they true Christians, or not? Secondly, What is meant by "falling away"? And thirdly, What is intended, when it is asserted, that it is impossible to renew them to repentance?

I. First, then, we answer the question, WHO ARE THE PEOPLE HERE SPOKEN OF? If you read Dr. Gill, Dr. Owen and almost all the eminent Calvinistic writers they all of them assert that these persons are not Christians. They say that enough is said here to represent a man who is a Christian externally but not enough to give the portrait of a true Believer. Now, it strikes me they would not have said this if they had not had some doctrine to uphold—for a child reading this passage would say that the persons intended by it must be Christians. If the Holy Spirit intended to describe Christians, I do not see that He could have used more explicit terms than there are here. How can a man be said to be enlightened, to taste of the heavenly gift and to be made partaker of the Holy Spirit, without being a child of God? With all deference to these learned doctors, and I admire and love them all, I humbly conceive that they allowed their judgments to be a little warped when they said that.

And I think I shall be able to show that none but true Believers are here described. First, they are spoken of as having been once enlightened. This refers to the enlightening influence of God's Spirit, poured into the soul at the time of conviction—when man is enlightened with regard to his spiritual state. When he is made to see how evil and bitter a thing it is to sin against God, made to feel how utterly powerless he is to rise from the grave of his corruption—and is further enlightened to see, that "by the deeds of the Law shall no flesh living be justified," and to behold Christ on the Cross, as the sinner's only hope.

The first work of grace is to enlighten the soul. By nature we are entirely dark. The Spirit, like a lamp, sheds light into the dark heart, revealing its corruption, displaying its sad state of destitution and, in due time, revealing also Jesus Christ, so that in His light we may see light. I cannot consider a man truly enlightened unless he is a child of God. Does not the term indicate a person taught of God? It is not the whole of Christian experience—but is it not a part?

Having enlightened us, as the text says, the next thing that God grants to us is a taste of the heavenly gift, by which we understand the heavenly gift of salvation, including the pardon of sin, justification by the imputed righteousness of Jesus Christ, regeneration by the Holy Spirit and all those gifts and graces in which the earlier dawn of spiritual life convey salvation. All true Believers have tasted of the heavenly gift. It is not enough for a man to be enlightened—the light may glare upon his eyeballs—and yet he may die—he must taste as well as see that the Lord is good. It is not enough to see that I am corrupt—I must taste that Christ is able to remove my corruption. It is not enough for me to know that He is the only Savior—I must taste of His flesh and of His blood and have a vital union with Him.

We most certainly think that when a man has been enlightened and has had an experience of grace, he is a Christian. Whatever those great divines might hold, we cannot think that the Holy Spirit would describe an unregenerate man as having been enlightened and as having tasted of the heavenly gift. No, my Brethren, if I have tasted of the heavenly gift, then that heavenly gift is mine. If I have had ever so short an experience of my Savior's love, I am one of His. If He has brought me into the green pastures and made me taste of the still waters and the tender grass, I need not fear as to whether I am really a child of God.

Then the Apostle gives a further description, a higher state of grace—sanctification by participation of the Holy Spirit. It is a peculiar privilege to Believers, after their first tasting of the heavenly gift, to be made partakers of the Holy Spirit. He is an indwelling Spirit. He dwells in the hearts, souls and minds of men. He makes this mortal flesh His home—He makes our soul His palace and there He rests. We do assert (and we think on the authority of Scripture), that no man can be a partaker of the Holy Spirit and yet be unregenerate. Where the Holy Spirit dwells there must be life and if I have participation with the Holy Spirit and fellowship with Him, then I may rest assured that my salvation has been purchased by the blood of the Savior. You need not fear, Beloved—if you have the Holy Spirit, you have that which ensures your salvation. If you, by an inward communion, can participate in His Spirit and if by a perpetual indwelling the Holy Spirit rests in you, you are not only a Christian, but you have arrived at some maturity in and by grace. You have gone beyond mere enlightenment—you have passed from the bare taste—you have attained to a positive feast and a partaking of the Holy Spirit.

Lest there should be any mistake, however, about the persons being children of God, the Apostle goes to a further stage of grace. They "have tasted the good Word of God." Now I will venture to say there are some good Christian people here who have tasted the heavenly gift, who have never "tasted the good Word of God." I mean by that, that they are really converted, have tasted the heavenly gift, but have not grown so strong in grace as to know the sweetness, the richness and the fatness of the very Word that saved them. They have been saved by the Word—but they have not come yet to realize, love and feed upon the Word as many others have.

It is one thing for God to work a work of grace in the soul—it is quite another thing for God to show us that work. It is one thing for the Word to work in us—it is another thing for us really and habitually to relish, taste and rejoice in that Word. Some of my hearers are true Christians but they have not got to that stage wherein they can love election and suck it down as a sweet morsel. They have not got wherein they can take the great doctrines of grace and feed upon them. But these people had. They had tasted the good Word of God as well as received the good gift—they had attained to such a state that they had loved the Word, had tasted and feasted upon it. It was the man of their right hand. They had counted it sweeter than honey, yes, sweeter than the droppings of the honeycomb. They had "tasted the good Word of God." I say again, if these people are not Believers—who are?

And they had gone further still. They had attained the summit of piety. They had received "the powers of the world to come." Not miraculous gifts which are denied us in these days but all those powers with which the Holy Spirit endows a Christian. And what are they? Why, there is the power of faith, which commands even the heavens themselves to rain and they rain, or stop the bottles of Heaven, that they rain not. There is the power of prayer, which puts a ladder between earth and Heaven and bids angels walk up and down, to convey our wants to God and bring down blessings from above. There is the power with which God girds His servant when he speaks by inspiration, which enables him to instruct others and lead them to Jesus. And whatever other power there may be—the power of holding communion with God, or the power of patiently waiting for the Son of Man—they were possessed by these individuals.

They were not simply children, but they were MEN—they were not merely alive but they were entitled with power. They were men whose muscles were firmly set, whose bones were strong. They had become giants in grace and had received not only the light, but the power also of the world to come. These, we say, whatever the meaning of the text must have been, were beyond a doubt none other than true and real Christians.

II. And now we answer the second question, WHAT IS MEANT BY FALLING AWAY? We must remind our friends that there is a vast distinction between falling away and falling. It is nowhere said in Scripture that if a man fall he cannot be renewed. On the contrary, "the righteous falls seven times, but he rises up again." And however many times the child of God does fall, the Lord still holds the righteous. Yes, when our bones are broken He binds up our bones again and sets us once more upon a rock. He says, "Return, you backsliding children of men, for I am married unto you," and if the Christian does backslide ever so far, still Almighty mercy cries, "Return, return, return and seek an injured Father's heart." He still calls His children back again.

Falling is not falling away. Let me explain the difference. A man who falls may behave just like a man who falls away and yet there is a great distinction between the two. I can use no better illustration than the distinction between fainting and dying. There lies a young creature—she can scarcely breathe—she cannot, herself, lift up her hand and if lifted up by anyone else, it falls. She is cold and stiff, she is faint, but not dead. There is another one, just as cold and stiff as she is, but there is this difference—she is dead. The Christian may faint and may fall down in a faint, too. And some may pick him up and say he is dead—but he is not. If he falls, God will lift him up again, but if he falls away, God Himself cannot save him. For it is impossible, if the righteous fall away, "to renew them again unto repentance."

Moreover, to fall away is not to commit sin under a temporary surprise and temptation. Abraham goes to Egypt. He is afraid that his wife will be taken away from him and he says, "She is my sister." That was a sin under a temporary surprise—a sin, of which, by-and-by he repented and God forgave him. Now that is falling—but it is not falling away. Even Noah might commit a sin which has degraded his memory even till now and shall disgrace it to the latest time—but, doubtless, Noah repented and was saved by Sovereign Grace. Noah fell, but Noah did not fall away. A Christian may go astray once and speedily return again—and though it is a sad, woeful and evil thing to be surprised into a sin—yet there is a great difference between this and the sin which would be occasioned by a total falling away from grace.

Nor can a man who commits a sin which is not exactly a surprise, be said to fall away. I believe that some Christian men—(God forbid that we should say much of it!—let us cover the nakedness of our brother with a cloak)—but I do believe that there are some Christians, who, for a period of time, have wandered into sin and yet have not positively fallen away. There is that black case of David—a case which has puzzled thousands. Certainly for some months David lived without making a public confession of his sin, but, doubtless, he had achings of heart, for grace had not ceased its work. There was a spark among the ashes that Nathan stirred up which showed that David was not dead, or else the match which the Prophet applied would not have caught light so readily. And so, Beloved, you may have wandered into sin for a time and gone far from God—and yet you are not the character here described, concerning whom it is said that it is impossible you should be saved. Wanderer though you are, you are your Father's son still, and mercy cries, "Repent, repent! Return unto your first husband, for then it was better with you than it is now. Return, O Wanderer, return."

Again, falling away is not even a giving up of profession. Some will say, "Now there is So-and-So, he used to make a profession of Christianity and now he denies it—and what is worse, he dares to curse and swear and says that he never knew Christ at all. Surely he must be fallen away." My Friend, he has fallen, fallen fearfully and fallen woefully—but I remember a case in Scripture of a man who denied his Lord and Master before His own face! You remember his name—he is an old friend of yours—our friend Simon Peter! He denied Him with oaths and curses and said, "I say unto you that I know not the man." And yet Jesus looked on Simon. He had fallen, but he had not fallen away—for, only two or three days after that, there was Peter at the tomb of his Master running there to meet his Lord, to be one of the first to find Him risen!

Beloved, you may even have denied Christ by open profession and yet if you repent there is mercy for you. Christ has not cast you away, you shall repent yet. You have not fallen away. If you had, I might not preach to you—for it is impossible for those who have fallen away to be renewed again unto repentance.

But someone says, "What is falling away?" Well, there never has been a case of it yet and therefore I cannot describe it from observation. But I will tell you what I suppose it is. To fall away would be for the Holy Spirit entirely to go out of a man—for His grace entirely to cease—not to lie dormant, but to cease to be—for God, who has begun a good work, to leave off doing it entirely—to take His hand completely and entirely away and say, "there, Man! I have half-saved you, now I will damn you." That is what falling away is.

It is not to sin temporarily. A child may sin against his father and still be alive. Falling away is like cutting the child's head off clean. Not falling merely, for then our Father could pick us up—but being dashed down a precipice where we are lost forever. Falling away would involve God's grace changing its living nature, God's immutability becoming variable, God's faithfulness becoming changeable and God Himself being undeified—for all these things falling away would necessitate.

III. But if a child of God could fall away and grace could cease in a man's heart—now comes the third question—Paul says, IT IS IMPOSSIBLE FOR HIM TO BE RENEWED. What did the Apostle mean? One eminent commentator says he meant that it would be very hard. It would be very hard, indeed, for a man who fell away, to be saved. But we reply, "My dear Friend, it does not say anything about its being very hard—it says it is impossible and we like to read our Bible just as a child would read it." It says it is impossible and we say that it would be utterly impossible, if such a case as is supposed were to happen—impossible for man and also impossible for God—for God has purposed that He never will grant a second salvation to save those whom the first salvation has failed to deliver.

Methinks, however, I hear someone say, "It seems to me that it is possible for some such to fall away," because it says, 'It is impossible, if they shall fall away, to renew them again into repentance.' " Well, my Friend, I will grant you your theory for a moment. You are a good Christian this morning. Let us apply it to yourself and see how you will like it. You have believed in Christ and committed your soul to God and you think that in some unlucky hour you may fall entirely away. Mark you, if you come to me and tell me that you have fallen away, how would you like me to say to you, "My Friend, you are as much damned as the devil in Hell! For it is impossible to renew you to repentance"?

"Oh, no, Sir," you would say, "I will repent again and join the Church." That is just the Arminian theory all over—but it is not in God's Scripture. If you once fall away you are as damned as any man who suffers in the gulf forever. And yet we have heard a man talk about people being converted three, four, and five times, and regenerated over and over again. I remember a good man (I suppose he was) pointing to a man who was walking along the street and saying, "That man has been born again three times, to my certain knowledge," (I could mention the name of the individual but I refrain from doing so) "and believe he will fall again," said he. "He is so much addicted to drinking that I do not believe the grace of God will do anything for him, unless he becomes a teetotaler."

Now, such men cannot read the Bible, because in case their members do positively fall away, here it is stated as a positive fact that it is impossible to renew them again unto repentance. But I ask my Arminian friend, does he not believe that as long as there is life there is hope? "Yes," he says—

"While the lamp holds out to burn,
The vilest sinner may return."

Well, that is not very consistent—to say this—and in the very next breath tell us that there are some people who fall away and consequently fall into such a condition that they cannot be saved. I want to know how you make these two things fit each other? I want you to make these two doctrines agree and until some enterprising individual will bring the north pole and set it on the top of the south, I cannot tell how you will accomplish it. The fact is you are quite right in saying, "While there is life there is hope"—but you are wrong in saying that any individual ever did fall into such a condition that it was impossible for him to be saved.

We come now to do two things—first to prove the doctrine, that if a Christian falls away, he cannot be saved. And, secondly, to improve the doctrine, or to show its use.

1. Now I am going to prove the doctrine that if a Christian FALL AWAY—not fall—for you understand how I have explained that—but if a Christian ceases to be a child of God and if grace dies out in his heart—he is then beyond the possibility of salvation and it is impossible for him ever to be renewed. Let me show you why.

First, it is utterly impossible, if you consider the work which has already broken down. When men have built bridges across streams, if they have been built of the strongest material and in the most excellent manner and yet the foundation has been found so bad that none will stand, what do they say? Why, "We have already tried the best which engineering or architecture has taught us, the best has already failed. We know nothing that can exceed what has been tried. And we do, therefore, feel that there remains no possibility of ever bridging that stream, or ever running a line of railroad across this bog or this morass, for we have already tried what is acknowledged to be the best scheme."

As the Apostle says, "These people have been once enlightened. They have had once the influence of the Holy Spirit revealing to them their sin—what now remains to be tried? They have been once convicted—is there anything superior to conviction? Does the Bible promise that the poor sinner shall have anything over and above the conviction of his sin to make him sensible of it? Is there anything more powerful than the sword of the Spirit? If that has not pierced the man's heart—is there anything else which will do it? Here is a man who has been under the hammer of God's Law but that has not broken his heart—can you find anything stronger? The lamp of God's Spirit has already lit up the caverns of his soul—if that is not sufficient, where will you borrow another?

Ask the sun—has he a lamp more bright than the illumination of the Spirit? Ask the stars—have they a light more brilliant than the light of the Holy Spirit?

Creation answers No. If that fails, then there is nothing else. These people, moreover, had tasted the heavenly gift—and though they had been pardoned and justified, yet pardon through Christ and justification were not enough (on this supposition) to save them. How else can they be saved? God has cast them away. After He has failed in saving them by these, what else can deliver them? Already they have tasted of the heavenly gift—is there a greater mercy for them? Is there a brighter dress than the robe of Christ's righteousness? Is there a more efficacious bath than that "fountain filled with blood"? No. All the earth echoes, "No." If the one has failed, what else does there remain?

These persons, too, have been partakers of the Holy Spirit—if that fails what more can we give them? If, my Hearer, the Holy Spirit dwells in your soul and that Holy Spirit does not sanctify you and keep you to the end, what else can be tried? Ask the blasphemer whether he knows a being, or dares to suppose a being superior to the Holy Spirit! Is there a being greater than Omnipotence? Is there a might greater than that which dwells in the Believer's new-born heart? And if already the Holy Spirit has failed, O, Heaven, tell us where we can find anything that can excel His might?

If that is ineffectual, what next is to be tried? These people, who had "tasted the good Word of Life," had loved the doctrines of grace. Those doctrines had entered into their souls and they had fed upon them. What new doctrines shall be preached to them? Prophet of ages! Where will you find another system of Divinity? Who shall we have? Shall we raise up Moses from the tomb?

Shall we fetch up all the ancient seers and bid them prophesy? If, then, there is only one doctrine that is true and if these people have fallen away after receiving that, how can they be saved?

Again, these people, according to the text, have had "the powers of the world to come." They have had power to conquer sin—power in faith, power in prayer, power of communion. With what greater power shall they be endowed? This has already failed—what next can be done? O you angels! Answer, what next? What other means remain? What else can avail, if already the great things of salvation have been defeated? What else shall now be attempted? He had been once saved—but yet it is supposed that he is lost. How, then, can he now be saved? Is there a supplementary salvation? Is there something that shall overtop Christ and be a Christ where Jesus is defeated?

And then the Apostle says that the greatness of their sin which they would incur, if they did fall away, would put them beyond the bounds of mercy. Christ died and by His death He made an atonement for His own murderers. He made an atonement for those sins which crucified Him once, but do we read that Christ will ever die for those who crucify Him twice? But the Apostle tells us that if Believers do fall away, they will "crucify the Son of God afresh and put Him to an open shame." Where, then, would be an atonement for that? He has died for me. What? Though the sins of all the world were on my shoulders, still they only crucified Him once and that one crucifixion has taken all those sins away. But if I crucified Him again, where would I find pardon? Could heavens, could earth, could Christ

Himself with His heart full of love, point me to another Christ—show to me a second Calvary—give me a second Gethsemane? Ah, no! The very guilt itself would put us beyond the pale of hope, if we were to fall away!

Again Beloved, think what it would necessitate to save such a man. Christ has died for him once, yet he has fallen away and is lost. The Spirit has regenerated him once and that regenerating work has been of no use. God has given him a new heart (I am only speaking, of course, on the supposition of the Apostle)—He has put His Law in that heart—yet He has departed from him—contrary to the promise that He should not. He has made him "like a shining light," but he did not "shine more and more unto the perfect day," he shone only unto blackness. What next? There must be a second incarnation, a second Calvary, a second Holy Spirit, a second regeneration, a second justification, although the first was finished and complete—in fact, I know not what. It would necessitate the upsetting of the whole kingdom of nature and grace and it would, indeed, be a world turned upside down, if after the gracious Savior failed, He were to attempt the work again.

If you read the 7th and 8th verses, you will see that the Apostle calls nature in to his assistance. He says, "The earth which drinks in the rain that comes often upon it and brings forth herbs meet for them by whom it is dressed, receives blessing from God: But that which bears thorns and briars is rejected and is nigh unto cursing; whose end it is to be burned." Look! There is a field. The rain comes on it and it brings forth good fruit. Well, then, there is God's blessing on it. But there is, according to your supposition, another field on which the same rain descends, which the same dew moistens. It has been plowed and harrowed as well as the other and the farmer has exercised all his craft upon it and yet it is not fertile.

Well, if the rain of Heaven did not fertilize it, what next? Already all the arts of agriculture have been tried, every implement has been worn out on its surface and yet it has been of no avail. What next? There remains nothing but that it shall be burned and cursed—given up like the desert of Sahara and resigned to destruction. So, my Hearer, could it be possible that grace could work in you and then not affect your salvation? That the influence of Divine Grace could come down, like rain from Heaven and yet return unto God void? There could not be any hope for you, for you would be "nigh unto cursing," and your end would be "to be burned."

There is one idea which has occurred to us. It has struck us as a singular thing that our Friends should hold that men can be converted, made into new creatures, then fall away and be converted again. I am an old creature by nature. God creates me into a new thing. He makes me a new creature. I cannot go back into an old creature for I cannot be uncreated. But yet, supposing that new creatureship of mine is not good enough to carry me to Heaven. What is to come after that? Must there be something above a new creature—a new, new creature? Really, my Friends, we have got into the country of Dreamland—but we were forced to follow our opponents into that region of absurdity for we do not know how else to deal with them.

And one thought more. There is nothing in Scripture which teaches us that there is any salvation, save the one salvation of Jesus Christ—nothing that tells us of any other power, super-excellent and surpassing the power of the Holy Spirit. These things have already been tried on the man and yet, according to the supposition, they have failed, for he has fallen away. Now God has never revealed a supplementary salvation for men on whom one salvation has had no effect. And until we are pointed to one Scripture which declares this, we will still maintain that the doctrine of the text is this—that if grace is ineffectual, if grace does not keep a man, then there is nothing left but that he must be damned. And what is that but to say, only going a little round about, that grace will do it? So that these words instead of militating against the Calvinistic doctrine of final perseverance, form one of the firmest proofs of it that could be afforded.

And now, lastly, we come to clarify this doctrine. If Christians can fall away and cease to be Christians, they cannot be renewed again to repentance. "But," says one, "You say they cannot fall away. What is the use of putting this 'if' in, like a bugbear to frighten children, or like a ghost that can have no existence?" My learned Friend, "Who are you that replies against God?" If God has put it in, He has put it in for wise reasons and for excellent purposes. Let me show you why.

First, O Christian, it is put in to keep you from falling away. God preserves His children from falling away. But He keeps them by the use of means—and one of these is the terrors of the Law—showing them what would happen if they were to fall away. There is a deep precipice—what is the best way to keep anyone from going down there? Why to tell him that if he did he would inevitably be dashed to pieces. In some old castle there is a deep cellar where there is a vast amount of fixed air and gas which would kill anybody who went down. What does the guide say?

"If you go down you will never come up alive." Who thinks of going down? The very fact of the guide telling us what the consequences would be, keeps us from it. Our Friend puts away from us a cup of arsenic, he does not want us to drink it, but he says, "If you drink it, it will kill you." Does he suppose for a moment that we should drink it? No. He tells us the consequence and he is sure we will not do it. So God says, "My child, if you fall over this precipice you will be dashed to pieces." What does the child do? He says, "Father, keep me. Hold me up and I shall be safe." It leads the Believer to greater dependence on God, to a holy fear and caution, because he knows that if he were to fall away he could not be renewed and he stands far away from that great gulf, because he knows that if he were to fall into it there would be no salvation for him.

It is calculated to excite fear and this holy fear keeps the Christian from falling. If I thought as the Arminian thinks, that I might fall away and then return again, I should pretty often fall away. For sinful flesh and blood would think it very nice to fall away and be a sinner—go and see the play at the theater, or get drunk—and then come back to the Church and be received again as a dear Brother who had fallen away for a little while. No doubt the minister would say, "Our Brother Charles is a little unstable at times." A little unstable?! He does not know anything about grace—for grace engenders a holy caution, because we feel that if we were not preserved by Divine power we should perish.

We tell our friend to put oil in his lamp, that it may continue to burn! Does that imply that it will be allowed to go out? No, God will give him oil to pour into the lamp continually. Like John Bunyan's figure—there was a fire and he saw a man pouring water upon it. "Now," says the Preacher, "don't you see that fire would go out, that water is calculated to put it out and if it does, it will never be lighted again?" But God does not permit that! For there is a man behind the wall who is pouring oil on the fire—and we have cause for gratitude in the fact that if the oil were not put in by a heavenly hand, we should inevitably be driven to destruction. Take care, then Christian, for this is a caution.

2. It is to excite our gratitude. Suppose you say to your little boy, "Don't you know, Tommy, if I were not to give you your dinner and your supper you would die? There is nobody else to give Tommy dinner and supper." What then?

The child does not think that you are not going to give him his dinner and supper—he knows you will—and he is grateful to you for them. The chemist tells us that if there were no oxygen mixed with the air, animals would die. Do you suppose that there will be no oxygen and therefore we shall die? No, he only teaches you the great wisdom of God, in having mixed the gases in their proper proportions.

Says one of the old astronomers, "There is great wisdom in God, that He has put the sun exactly at a right distance—not so far away that we should be frozen to death and not so near that we should be scorched." He says, "If the sun were a million miles nearer to us we should be scorched to death." Does the man suppose that the sun will be a million miles nearer, and, therefore, we shall be scorched to death? He says, "If the sun were a million miles farther off we should be frozen to death." Does he mean that the sun will be a million miles farther off, and therefore we shall be frozen to death? Not at all. Yet it is quite a rational way of speaking to show us how grateful we should be to God. So says the Apostle. Christian—if you should fall away, you could never be renewed unto repentance—then, by His grace, He keeps you—

"See a stone that hangs in air,
see a spark in ocean live:
Kept alive with death so near,
I to God the glory give."

There is a cup of sin which would damn your soul, O Christian. Oh, what grace is that which holds your arm and will not let you drink it? There you are, at this hour, like the bird-catcher of St. Kilda—you are being drawn to Heaven by a single rope—if that hand which holds you let you go, if that rope which grasps you breaks—you are dashed on the rocks of damnation. Lift up your heart to God, then, and bless Him that His arm is not wearied and is never shortened that it cannot save. Lord Kenmure, when he was dying, said to Rutherford, "Man! My name is written on Christ's hand and I see it!

That is bold talk, Man, but I see it!" Then, if that is the case, His hand must be severed from His body before my name can be taken from Him. And if it is engraved on His heart, His heart must be rent out before they can rend my name out.

Hold on, then and trust, Believer! You have an anchor of the soul both sure and steadfast, which enters within the veil—the winds are bellowing, the tempests howling—should the cable slip, or your anchor break, you are lost. See those rocks on which myriads are driving?—You are wrecked there if grace leaves you. See those depths in which the skeletons of sailors sleep?—You are there if that anchor fails you. It would be impossible to moor you again, if once that anchor broke, for there are no other anchors. There can be no other salvation—if that one fails you, it is impossible that you ever should be saved. Therefore thank God that you have an Anchor that cannot fail and then loudly sing—

"How can I sink with such a prop,
As my eternal God
Who bears the earth's huge pillars up,
And spreads the heavens abroad?

How can I die, when Jesus lives?
Who rose and left the dead?
Pardon and grace my soul receives
From my exalted Head."

Sermon No. 1735
Delivered on August 19th, 1883
by Rev. C. H. Spurgeon
at Exeter Hall

THE DOCTRINES OF GRACE DO NOT LEAD TO SIN

"For sin shall not have dominion over you: for you are not under the Law, but under Grace. What then? Shall we sin, because we are not under the Law, but under Grace? God forbid."

—Romans 6:14, 15

LAST Sabbath morning I tried to show that the substance and essence of the true Gospel is the Doctrine of God's Grace [A Gospel Worth Dying For—No. 1734, Volume 29]—that, in fact, if you take away the Grace of God from the Gospel you have extracted from it its very life-blood and there is nothing left worth preaching, worth believing, or worth contending for. Grace is the soul of the Gospel—without it the Gospel is dead. Grace is the music of the Gospel—without it the Gospel is silent as to all comfort. I also endeavored to set forth the Doctrine of Grace in brief terms, teaching that God deals with sinful men upon the footing of pure mercy—finding them guilty and condemned, He gives free pardons, altogether irrespective of past character, or of any good works which may be foreseen. Moved only by pity, He devises a plan for their rescue from sin and its consequences—a plan in which Grace is the leading feature.

Out of free favor He has provided, in the death of His dear Son, an atonement by means of which His mercy can be justly bestowed. He accepts all those who place their trust in this Atonement, selecting faith as the way of salvation, that it may be all of Grace. In this He acts, from a motive found within Himself, and not because of any reason found in the sinner's conduct—past, present, or future. I tried to show that this Grace of God flows towards the sinner from of old and begins its operations upon him when there is nothing good in him—it works in him that which is good and acceptable—and continues so to work in him till the deed of Grace is complete and the Believer is received up into the glory for which he is made meet.

Grace commences to save and it perseveres till all is done. From first to last, from the "A" to the "Z" of the heavenly alphabet, everything in salvation is of Grace and Grace alone! All is of free favor, nothing of merit. "By Grace are you saved through faith; and that not of yourselves; it is the gift of God." "So then it is not of him that wills, nor of him that runs, but of God that shows mercy." No sooner is this doctrine set forth in a clear light than men begin to quibble with it. It is the target for all carnal logic to shoot at. Unrenewed minds never liked it and they never will—it is too humbling to human pride, making light of the nobility of human nature. That men are to be saved by Divine charity; that they must, as condemned criminals, receive pardon by the exercise of the royal prerogative or else perish in their sins is a teaching which they cannot endure!

God alone is exalted in the sovereignty of His mercy—the sinner can do no better than meekly touch the silver scepter and accept undeserved favor just because God wills to give it! This is not pleasant to the great minds of our philosophers and the broad phylacteries of our moralists and, therefore, they turn aside and fight against the empire of Grace. Straightway the unrenewed man seeks out artillery with which to fight against the Gospel of the Grace of God! And one of the biggest guns he has ever brought to the front is the declaration that the Doctrines of the Grace of God must lead to licentiousness! If great sinners are freely saved, then men will more readily become great sinners—and if, when God's Grace regenerates a man, it abides with him, then men will infer that they may live as they like and yet be saved.

This is the constantly repeated objection which I have heard till it wearies me with its vain and false noise. I am almost ashamed to have to refute so rotten an argument! They dare to assert that men will take license to be guilty because God is gracious! And they do not hesitate to say that if men are not to be saved by their works, they will come to the conclusion that their conduct is a matter of indifference and that they may as well sin that Grace may abound! This morning I want to talk a little about this notion, for in part it is a great mistake and in part it is a great lie. In part it is a mistake because it arises from misconception. And in part it is a lie because men know better, or might know better if they pleased.

I begin by admitting that the charge does appear somewhat probable. It does seem very likely that if we are to go up and down the country and say, "The very chief of sinners may be forgiven through believing in Jesus Christ, for God is displaying mercy to the very vilest of the vile," then sin will seem to be a cheap thing. If we are everywhere to cry, "Come, you sinners, come and welcome, and receive free and immediate pardon through the Sovereign Grace of God," it does seem probable that some may basely reply, "Let us sin without ceasing, for we can easily obtain forgiveness." But that which looks to be probable is not, therefore, certain! On the contrary, the improbable and the unexpected full often come to pass. In questions of moral influence, nothing is more deceptive than theory. The ways of the human mind are not to be laid down with a pencil and compasses—man is a singular being.

Even that which is logical is not always inevitable, for men's minds are not governed by the rules of the schools. I believe that the inference which would lead men to sin because Grace reigns is not logical, but the very reverse—and I venture to assert that, as a matter of fact, ungodly men do not, as a rule, plead the Grace of God as an excuse for their sin! As a rule they are too indifferent to care about reasons at all! And if they do offer an excuse, it is usually more flimsy and superficial. There may be a few men of perverse minds who have used this argument, but there is no accounting for the freaks of the fallen understanding. I shrewdly suspect that in any cases in which such reasoning has been put forward, it was a mere pretense and by no means a plea which satisfied the sinner's own conscience.

If men do excuse themselves, it is generally in some veiled manner, for the most of them would be utterly ashamed to state the argument in plain terms. I question whether the devil himself would be found reasoning thus—"God is merciful, therefore let us be more sinful." It is so diabolical an inference that I do not like to charge my fellow men with it, though our moralist opposers do not hesitate thus to degrade themselves! Surely, no intelligent being can really persuade itself that the goodness of God is a reason for offending Him more than ever! Moral insanity produces strange reasoning, but it is my solemn conviction that very rarely do men practically consider the Grace of God to be a motive for sin. That which seems so probable at the first blush is not so when we come to consider it.

I have admitted that a few human beings have turned the Grace of God into lasciviousness, but I trust no one will ever argue against any doctrine on account of the perverse use made of it by the baser sort. Cannot every Truth of God be perverted? Is there a single doctrine of Scripture which graceless hands have not twisted into mischief? Is there not an almost infinite ingenuity in wicked men for making evil out of good? If we are to condemn a Truth because of the misbehavior of individuals who profess to believe it, we would be found condemning our Lord, Himself, for what Judas did—

and our holy faith would die at the hands of apostates and hypocrites!

Let us act like rational men. We do not find fault with ropes because poor insane creatures have hanged themselves with them! Nor do we ask that the wares of Sheffield may be destroyed because edged tools are the murderer's instruments. It may appear probable that the Doctrine of Free Grace will be made into a license for sin, but a better acquaintance with the curious working of the human mind corrects the notion. Fallen as human nature is, it is still human and, therefore, does not take kindly to certain forms of evil—such, for instance, as inhuman ingratitude. It is hardly human to multiply injuries upon those who return us continued benefits.

The case reminds me of the story of half-a-dozen boys who had severe fathers, accustomed to flogging them within an inch of their lives. Another boy was with them who was tenderly beloved by his parents and known to be so. These young gentlemen met together to hold a council of war about robbing an orchard. They were, all of them, anxious to get about it except the favored youth who did not agree with the proposal. One of them cried out, "You need not be afraid! If our fathers catch us at this work, we shall be half-killed, but your father won't lay a hand upon you." The little boy answered, "And do you think because my father is kind to me, that therefore I will do wrong and grieve him? I will do nothing of the sort to my dear father! He is so good to me that I cannot vex him."

It would appear that the argument of the many boys was not overpoweringly convincing to their companion—the opposite conclusion was quite as logical and evidently carried weight with it. If God is good to the undeserving, some men will go into sin, but there are others of a nobler order whom the goodness of God leads to repentance. They scorn the beast-like argument that the more loving God is, the more rebellious we may be—and they feel that against the God of Goodness it is an evil thing to rebel. By the way, I cannot help observing that I have known persons object to the evil influence of the Doctrines of Grace who were by no means qualified, by their own morality, to be judges of the subject! Morals must be in a poor way when immoral persons become their guardians!

The doctrine of Justification by Faith is frequently objected to as injurious to morals. A newspaper, sometime ago, quoted a verse from a popular hymn—

Weary, working, plodding one,
Why toil you so?
Cease your doing; all was done
Long, long ago!

'Till to Jesus' work you cling
By a simple faith,
Doing' is a deadly thing,
Doing' ends in death."

This is styled mischievous teaching! When I read the article, I felt a deep interest in this corrector of Luther and Paul, and I wondered how much he had drunk in order to elevate his mind to such a pitch of theological knowledge! I have found men pleading against the Doctrines of Grace on the ground that they did not promote morality, to whom I could have justly replied,

"What has morality to do with you, or you with it?" These sticklers for good works are not often the doers of them! Let legalists look to their own hands and tongues—and leave the Gospel of Grace and its advocates to answer for themselves!

Looking back in history, I see upon its pages a refutation of the oft-repeated calumny. Who dares to suggest that the men who believed in the Grace of God have been sinners above other sinners? With all their faults, those who throw stones at them will be few if they first prove themselves to be their superiors in character, when have they been the patrons of vice, or the defenders of injustice? Pitch upon the point in English history when this doctrine was very strong in the land—who were the men that held these doctrines most firmly? Men like Owen, Charnock, Manton, Howe! And I hesitate not to add Oliver Cromwell! What kind of men were these? Did they pander to the licentiousness of a court? Did they invent a Book of Sports for Sabbath Diversion? Did they haunt ale-houses and places of revelry?

Every historian will tell you the greatest fault of these men, in the eyes of their enemies, was that they were too precise for the generation in which they lived—so they called them Puritans and condemned them as holding a gloomy theology! Sirs, if there was iniquity in the land in that day, it was to be found with the theological party which preached up salvation by works! The gentlemen with their womanish locks and perfumed hair, whose speech savored of profanity, were the advocates of salvation by works and, all bedabbled with lust, they pleaded for human merit!

But the men who believed in Grace alone were of another style. They were not in the chambers of rioting and wantonness! Where were they? They might be found on their knees crying to God for help in temptation and in persecuting times they might be found in prison, cheerfully suffering the loss of all things for the Truth of God's sake! The Puritans were the godliest men on the face of the earth! Are men so inconsistent as to nickname them for their purity and yet say that their doctrines lead to sin? Nor is this a solitary instance—this instance of Puritanism—all history confirms the rule and when it is said that these doctrines will create sin, I appeal to facts, and leave the oracle to answer as it may. If we are ever to see a pure and godly England, we must have a gospelized England! If we are to put down drunkenness and the social evil, it must be by the proclamation of the Grace of God!

Men must be forgiven by the Grace of God, renewed by the Grace of God, transformed by the Grace of God, sanctified by the Grace of God and preserved by the Grace of God! And when that comes to pass, the golden age will dawn! But while they are merely taught their duty and left to do it of themselves in their own strength, it is labor in vain! You may flog a dead horse a long while before it will stir—you need to put life into it, or else all your flogging will fail. To teach men to walk who have no feet is poor work—and so is instruction in morals before Grace gives a heart to love holiness! The Gospel, alone, supplies men with motive and strength and, therefore, it is to the Gospel that we must look as the real reformer of men!

I shall fight, this morning, with the objection before us as I shall find strength. The Doctrines of Grace, the whole plan of salvation by Grace, is most promotive of holiness. Wherever it comes, it helps us to say, "God forbid," to the question, "Shall we sin, because we are not under the Law, but under Grace?" This I would set out in the clear sunlight. I wish to call your attention to some six or seven points.

I. First, you will see that the Gospel of the Grace of God promotes real holiness in men by remembering that THE SALVATION WHICH IT BRINGS IS SALVATION FROM THE POWER OF SIN. When we preach salvation to the vilest of men, some suppose we mean by that a mere deliverance from Hell and an entrance into Heaven. It includes all that and results in that, but that is not what we mean! What we mean by salvation is this—deliverance from the love of sin, rescue from the habit of sin, setting free from the desire to sin. Now listen. If it is so, that that gift of deliverance from sin is the gift of Divine Grace, in what way will that gift, or the free distribution of it, produce sin? I fail to see any such danger. On the contrary, I say to the man who proclaims a gracious promise of victory over sin, "Make all speed—go up and down throughout the world and tell the vilest of mankind that God is willing, by His Grace, to set them free from the love of sin and to make new creatures of them."

Suppose the salvation we preach is this—"You that have lived ungodly and wicked lives may enjoy your sins and yet escape the penalty"? That would be mischievous, indeed! But if it is this—"You that live the most ungodly and wicked lives may yet, by believing in the Lord Jesus, be enabled to change those lives so that you shall live unto God instead of serving sin and Satan"?—what harm can come to the most prudish morals? Why, I say spread such a Gospel and let it circulate through every part of our vast empire! Let all men hear it, whether they rule in the House of Lords or suffer in the house of bondage! Tell them everywhere that God freely and of infinite Grace is willing to renew men and women and make them new creatures in Christ Jesus! Can any evil consequences come of the freest proclamation of this news? The worse men are, the more gladly would we see them embracing this Truth of God, for these are they who most need it!

I say to every one of you, whoever you may be, whatever your past condition—God can renew you according to the power of His Grace so that you who are to Him like dead, dry bones, can be made to live by His Spirit! That renewal will be seen in holy thoughts, pure words and righteous acts to the glory of God. In great love He is prepared to work all these things in all who believe. Why should any man be angry at such a statement? What possible harm can come of it? I defy the most cunning adversary to object, upon the ground of morals, to God's giving men new hearts and right spirits even as He pleases!

II. Secondly, let it not be forgotten as a matter of fact that THE PRINCIPLE OF LOVE HAS BEEN FOUND TO POSSESS VERY GREAT POWER OVER MEN. In the infancy of history, nations dream that crime can be put down by severity and they rely upon fierce punishments—but experience corrects the error. Our forefathers dreaded forgery, which is a troublesome fraud that interferes with the confidence which should exist between man and man. To put it down, they made forgery a capital offense. Alas for the murders committed by that law! Yet the constant use of the gallows was never sufficient to stamp out the crime. Many offenses have been created and multiplied by the penalty which was meant to suppress them.

Some offenses have almost ceased when the penalty against them has been lightened. It is a notable fact as to men that if they are forbidden to do a thing, they straightway pine to do it, though they had never thought of doing it before! Law commands obedience, but does not promote it—it often creates disobedience—and an over-weighted penalty has been known to provoke an offense. Law fails, but love wins! Love in any case makes sin infamous. If one should rob another, it would be sufficiently bad. But suppose a man robbed his friend who had helped him often when he was in need? Everyone would say that his crime was most disgraceful. Love brands sin on the forehead with a red-hot iron. If a man should kill an enemy, the offense would be grievous, but if he slew his father, to whom he owes his life, or his mother, on whose breasts he was nursed in infancy, then all would cry out against the monster! In the light of love, sin is seen to be exceedingly sinful.

Nor is this all. Love has a great constraining power towards the highest form of virtue. Deeds to which a man could not be compelled on the ground of law, men have cheerfully done because of love. Would our brave seamen man the lifeboat to obey an Act of Parliament? No, they would indignantly revolt against being forced to risk their lives! But they will do it freely to save their fellow men. Remember that text of the Apostle, "Scarcely for a righteous (or merely just) man will one die: yet perhaps," says he, "for a good (benevolent) man some would even dare to die." Goodness wins the heart and one is ready to die for the kind and generous! Look how men have thrown away their lives for great leaders. That was an immortal saying of the wounded French soldier. When searching for the bullet the surgeon cut deeply and the patient cried out, "A little lower and you will touch the Emperor," meaning that the Emperor's name was written on his heart!

In several notable instances, men have thrown themselves into the jaws of death to save a leader whom they loved. Duty holds the fort, but love casts its body in the way of the deadly bullet! Who would think of sacrificing his life on the ground of law? Love alone counts not life so dear as the service of the Beloved! Love to Jesus creates a heroism of which law knows nothing. All the history of the Church of Christ, when it has been true to its Lord, is a proof of this. Kindness, also, working by the law of love, has often changed the most unworthy and therein proved that it is not a factor of evil. We have often heard the story of the soldier who had been reduced to the lowest rank, flogged and imprisoned—and yet for all that he would get drunk and misbehave himself.

The commanding officer said, one day, "I have tried almost everything with this man and can do nothing with him. I will try one more thing." When he was brought in, the officer addressed him and said, "You seem incorrigible—we have tried everything with you—there seems to be no hope of a change in your wicked conduct. I am determined to see if another plan will have any effect. Though you deserve flogging and long imprisonment, I shall freely forgive you." The man was greatly moved by the unexpected and undeserved pardon—and became a good soldier. The story wears truth on its brow—we all see that it would probably end so! That anecdote is such a good argument that I will give you another.

A drunkard woke up one morning from his drunken sleep with his clothes on him just as he had rolled down the night before. He saw his only child, his daughter, Millie, getting his breakfast. Coming to his senses, he said to her, "Millie, why do you stay with me?" She answered, "Because you are my father, and because I love you." He looked at himself and saw what a sottish, ragged, good-for-nothing creature he was, and he answered her, "Millie, do you really love me?" The child cried, "Yes, father, I do, and I will never leave you because when mother died she said, 'Millie, stick to your father and always pray for him, and one of these days he will give up drinking and be a good father to you'—so I will never leave you."

Is it wonderful when I add that, as the story has it, Millie's father cast away his drink and became a Christian man? It would have been more remarkable if he had not! Millie was trying Free Grace, was she not? According to our moralists she should have said, "Father, you are a horrible wretch! I have stuck to you long enough! I must now leave you, or else I shall be encouraging other fathers to get drunk." Under such proper dealing I fear Millie's father would have continued a drunkard till he drank himself into Hell. But the power of love made a better man of him. Do not these instances prove that undeserved love has a great influence for good?

Hear another story—In the old persecuting times, there lived in Cheapside one who feared God and attended the secret meetings of the saints. And near him there dwelt a poor cobbler whose needs were often relieved by the merchant. But the poor man was a cross-grained being and, most ungratefully, from hope of reward, laid an information against his kind friend on the score of religion. This accusation would have brought the merchant to death by burning if he had not found a means of escape. Returning to his house, the injured man did not change his generous behavior to the malignant cobbler, but, on the contrary, was more liberal than ever! The cobbler was, however, in an ill mood and avoided the good man with all his might, running away at his approach.

One day he was obliged to meet him face to face and the Christian man asked him, gently, "Why do you shun me? I am not your enemy. I know all that you did to injure me, but I never had an angry thought against you.

I have helped you and I am willing to do so as long as I live, only let us be friends." Do you marvel that they clasped hands? Would you wonder if, before long, the poor man was found at the Lollards' meeting? All such anecdotes rest upon the assured fact that Grace has a strange subduing power and leads men to goodness—drawing them with cords of love and bands of man! The Lord knows that bad as men are, the key of their hearts hangs on the nail of love. He knows that His almighty goodness, though often baffled, will triumph in the end!

I believe my point is proved. To myself it is so. However, we must pass on.

III. There is no fear that the Doctrines of Grace will lead men to sin, because THEIR OPERATIONS ARE CONNECTED WITH A SPECIAL REVELATION OF THE EVIL OF SIN. Iniquity is made to be exceedingly bitter before it is forgiven or when it is forgiven. When God begins to deal with a man with a view of blotting out his sins and making him His child, He usually causes him to see his evil ways in all their heinousness. He makes him look on sin with fixed eyes, till he cries with David, "My sin is ever before me!" In my own case, when under conviction of sin, no cheering object met my mental eye—my soul saw only darkness and a horrible tempest. It seemed as though a horrible spot were painted on my eyeballs!

Guilt, like a grim chamberlain, drew the curtains of my bed, so that I rested not, but in my slumbers anticipated the wrath to come. I felt that I had offended

God and that this was the most awful thing a human being could do. I was out of order with my Creator, out of order with the universe—I had damned myself forever—and I wondered that I did not immediately feel the gnawing of the undying worm. Even to this hour a sight of sin causes the most dreadful emotions in my heart. Any man or woman here who has passed through that experience, or anything like it, will always feel a deep horror of sin. A burnt child dreads the fire. "No," says the sinner to his tempter, "you once deceived me and I so smarted in consequence, but I will not again be deluded. I have been delivered, like a brand from the burning, and I cannot go back to the fire."

By the operations of Grace we are made weary of sin; we loathe both it and its imaginary pleasures. We would utterly exterminate it from the soil of our nature. It is a thing accursed, even as Amalek was to Israel. If you, my Friend, do not detest every sinful thing, I fear you are still in the gall of bitterness, for one of the sure fruits of the Spirit is a love of holiness and a loathing of every false way. A deep inward experience forbids the child of God to sin—he has known within himself its judgment and its condemnation and, therefore, it is a thing abhorrent to him. An enmity both fierce and endless exists between the chosen seed and the serpent brood of evil—therefore the fear that Grace will be abused is abundantly safeguarded.

IV. Remember, also, that not only is the forgiven man thus set against sin by the process of conviction, but EVERY MAN WHO TASTES OF THE SAVING

GRACE OF GOD IS MADE A NEW CREATURE IN CHRIST JESUS. Now if the Doctrines of Grace in the hands of an ordinary man might be dangerous, yet they would cease to be so in the hands of one who is quickened by the Spirit and created anew in the image of God. The Holy Spirit comes upon the chosen one and transforms him—his ignorance is removed, his affections are changed, his understanding is enlightened, his will is subdued, his desires refined, his life is changed—in fact, he is as one new-born, to whom all things have become new. This change is compared in Scripture to the resurrection from the dead, to a creation and to a new birth.

This takes place in every man who becomes a partaker of the Free Grace of God. "You must be born again," said Christ to Nicodemus, and gracious men are born again! One said the other day, "If I believed that I was eternally saved, I should live in sin." Perhaps you would—but if you were renewed in heart you would not! "But," says one, "if I believed God loved me from before the foundation of the world and that, therefore, I would be saved, I would take a full swing in sin." Perhaps you and the devil would, but God's regenerate children are not of so base a nature! To them, the abounding Grace of the Father is a bond to righteousness which they never think of breaking—they feel the sweet constraints of sacred gratitude and desire to perfect holiness in the fear of the Lord.

All beings live according to their nature and the regenerated man works out the holy instincts of his renewed mind! Crying after holiness, warring against sin, laboring to be pure in all things, the regenerate man puts forth all his strength towards that which is pure and perfect. A new heart makes all the difference! Given a new nature, all the propensities run in a different way, and the blessings of almighty love no longer involve peril, but suggest the loftiest aspirations!

V. One of the chief securities for the holiness of the pardoned is found in the way of CLEANSING THROUGH ATONEMENT. The blood of Jesus sanctifies as well as pardons. The sinner learns that his free pardon cost the life of his best Friend and, in order to his salvation the Son of God, Himself, agonized even to a bloody sweat and died forsaken of His God. This causes a sacred mourning for sin as he looks upon the Lord whom he pierced. Love to Jesus burns within the pardoned sinner's breast, for the Lord is his Redeemer and, therefore, he feels a burning indignation against the murderous evil of sin. To him all manner of evil is detestable since it is stained with the Savior's blood.

As the penitent sinner hears the cry of, "*Eloi, Sabachthani!*" he is horrified to think that One so pure and good should be forsaken of Heaven because of the sin which He bore in His people's place. From the death of Jesus the mind draws the conclusion that sin is exceedingly sinful in the sight of the Lord—for if eternal justice would not spare even the well-beloved Jesus when imputed sin was upon Him, how much less will it spare guilty men? It must be an unutterably thing full of poison which could make even the Immaculate Jesus suffer so terribly!

Nothing can be imagined which can have greater power over gracious minds than the vision of a crucified Savior denouncing sin by all His wounds—and by every falling drop of blood. What? Live in the sin which slew Jesus? Find pleasure in that which worked His death? Trifle with that which laid His Glory in the dust? Impossible! Thus you see that the gifts of Free Grace, when handed down by a pierced hand, are never likely to suggest self-indulgence in sin, but the very reverse.

VI. Sixthly, a man who becomes a partaker of Divine Grace and receives the new nature is ever afterwards A PARTAKER OF DAILY HELPS FROM GOD'S HOLY SPIRIT. God the Holy Spirit deigns to dwell in the bosom of every man whom God has saved by His Grace. Is not that a wonderful means of sanctifying? By what process can men be better kept from sin than by having the Holy Spirit, Himself, dwell as Vice-Regent within their hearts? The Ever-Blessed Spirit leads Believers to be much in prayer—and what a power for holiness is found in the child of Grace speaking to the heavenly Father! The tempted man flies to his chamber, unloads his grief on God, looks to the flowing wounds of his Redeemer and comes down strong to resist temptation.

The Divine Word, also, with its precepts and promises, is a never-failing source of sanctification. Were it not that we, every day, bathe in the sacred fountain of eternal strength, we might soon be weak and irresolute—but fellowship with God renews us in our vigorous warfare with sin. How is it possible that the Doctrines of Grace could suggest sin to men who constantly draw near to God? The renewed man is also, by God's Spirit, frequently quickened in conscience, so that things which, before, did not strike him as sinful, are seen in a clearer light and are, consequently, condemned. I know that certain matters are sinful to me, today, which did not appear so 10 years ago—my judgment has, I trust, been more and more cleared of the blindness of sin.

The natural conscience is callous and hard, but the gracious conscience grows more and more tender till, at last, it becomes as sensitive as a raw wound. He who has most Grace is most conscious of his need of more Grace. The gracious are often afraid to put one foot before another for fear of doing wrong. Have you not felt this holy fear, this sacred caution? It is by this means that the Holy Spirit prevents your ever turning your Christian liberty into licentiousness, or daring to make the Grace of God an argument for folly! Then, in addition to this, the good Spirit leads us into high and hallowed communion with God—and I defy any man to live upon the mount with God and then come down to transgress like men of the world! If you have walked the palace floor of Glory and seen the King in His beauty, till the light of His Countenance has been your Heaven, you cannot be content with the gloom and murkiness of the tents of wickedness!

To lie, to deceive, to feign, as the men of the world do, will no longer become you. You are of another race and your conversation is above them—"Your speech betrays you." If you do, indeed, dwell with God, the perfume of the ivory palaces will be about you and men will know that you have been in other haunts than theirs. If the child of God goes wrong in any degree, he loses, to some extent, the sweetness of his communion and only as he walks carefully with God does he enjoy full fellowship so that this rising or falling in communion becomes a sort of parental discipline in the house of the Lord. We have no court with a judge, but we have home with its fatherhood, its smile and its rod! We lack not for order in the family of love, for our Father deals with us as with sons. Thus, in a thousand ways, all danger of our presuming upon the Grace of God is effectually removed.

VII. THE ENTIRE ELEVATION OF THE MAN WHO IS MADE A PARTAKER OF THE GRACE OF GOD is also a special preservative against sin. I venture to say, though it may be controverted, that the man who believes the glorious Doctrines of Grace is usually a much higher style of man than the person who has no opinion upon the matter. What do most men think about? Bread and butter, house rent and clothes. But the men who consider the Doctrines of the Gospel muse upon the Everlasting Covenant, predestination, immutable love, effectual calling, God in Christ Jesus, the work of the Spirit, justification, sanctification, adoption and such noble themes! Why, it is a refreshment merely to look over the catalog of these grand Truths of God!

Others are as children playing with little sand heaps on the seashore. But the Believer in Free Grace walks among hills and mountains! The themes of thought around him tower upward, Alps on Alps! The man's mental stature rises with his surroundings and he becomes a thoughtful being, communing with sublimities. This is no small matter, for a thing so apt to grovel as the average human intellect! So far as deliverance from mean vices and degrading lusts must in this way be promoted, I say it is no small thing! Thoughtlessness is the prolific mother of sin! It is a hopeful sign when minds begin to roam among lofty Truths of God.

The man who has been taught of God to think, will not so readily sin as the being whose mind is buried beneath his flesh. The man has now obtained a different view of himself from that which led him to trifle away his time with the idea that there was nothing better for him than to be merry while he could. He says, "I am one of God's chosen, ordained to be His son, His heir, joint-heir with Jesus Christ! I am set apart to be a king and priest unto God and as such I cannot be godless, nor live for the common objectives of life." He rises in the objective of his pursuit—he cannot live unto himself, for he is not his own—he is bought with a price. Now he dwells in the Presence of God and life to him is real, earnest and sublime! He cares not to scrape together gold with the muck-rake of the covetous, for he is immortal and must seek eternal gains.

He feels that he is born for Divine purposes and enquires, "Lord, what would You have me to do?" He feels that God has loved him so that his love may flow forth to others. God's choice of any one man has a bearing upon all the rest—He elects a Joseph that a whole family, a whole nation, no, the whole world, may be preserved alive when famine had broken the staff of bread. We are, each one, as a lamp kindled that we may shine in the dark and light up other lamps. New hopes come crowding on the man who is saved by Grace. His immortal spirit enjoys glimpses of the endless. As God has loved him in time, he believes that the same love will bless him in eternity. He knows that his Redeemer lives and that in the latter days he shall behold Him and, therefore, he has no fear of the future.

Even while here below he begins to sing the songs of the angels, for his spirit spies from afar the dawn of the Glory which is yet to be revealed! Thus with joyous heart and light footsteps he goes forward to the unknown future as merrily as to a wedding feast! Is there a sinner here, a guilty sinner, one who has no merit, no claim to mercy whatever? Is there one willing to be saved by God's Free Grace through believing in Jesus Christ? Then let me tell you, Sinner, there is not a word in God's Book against you, not a line or syllable, but everything is in your favor! "This is a faithful saying, and worthy of all acceptation, that Christ Jesus came into the world to save sinners," even the chief! Jesus came into the world to save you! Only trust Him and rest in Him!

I will tell you what ought to fetch you to Christ at once—it is the thought of His amazing love! A profligate son had been a great grief to his father. He had robbed him and disgraced him and, at last, he ended by bringing his gray hairs with sorrow to the grave. He was a horrible wretch of a son—no one could have been more graceless! However, he attended his father's funeral and he stayed to hear the will read. Perhaps it was the chief reason why he was there. He had fully made up his mind that his father would cut him off with a shilling—and he meant to make it very unpleasant for the rest of the family. To his great astonishment, as the will was read, it ran something like this—"As for my son, Richard, though he has fearfully wasted my substance; and though he has often grieved my heart, I would have him know that I consider him to still be my own dear child and, therefore, in token of my undying love, I leave him the same share as the rest of his brothers."

He left the room. He could not stand it. The surprising love of his father had mastered him! He came down to the executor the next morning and said, "You surely did not read correctly?" "Yes I did. there it stands." "Then," he said, "I feel ready to curse myself that I ever grieved my dear old father. Oh, that I could fetch him back again!" Love was born in that base heart by an unexpected display of love. May not your case be similar? Our Lord Jesus Christ is dead, but He has left in His will that the chief of sinners are objects of His choicest mercy! Dying, He prayed, "Father, forgive them." Risen, He pleads for transgressors. Sinners are always on His mind—their salvation is His great objective. His blood is for them, His heart for them, His righteousness for them, His Heaven for them!

Come, O you guilty ones, and receive your legacy! Put out the hand of faith and grasp your portion! Trust Jesus with your souls and He will save you! God bless you. Amen.

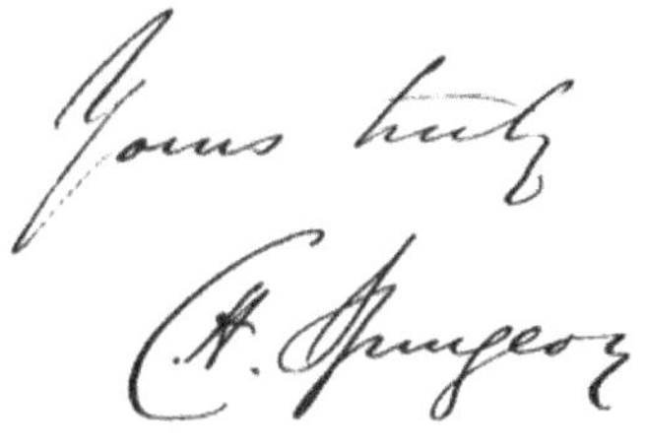

ABOUT THE AUTHOR

CHARLES HADDON (C.H.) SPURGEON (June 19, 1834 – January 31, 1892) was a British Particular Baptist preacher. Spurgeon remains highly influential among Christians of different denominations, among whom he is known as the "Prince of Preachers". He was a strong figure in the Reformed Baptist tradition, defending the Church in agreement with the 1689 London Baptist Confession of Faith understanding, and opposing the liberal and pragmatic theological tendencies in the Church of his day.

In his lifetime, Spurgeon preached to around 10,000,000 people, often up to 10 times each week at different places. Spurgeon was the pastor of the congregation of the New Park Street Chapel (later the Metropolitan Tabernacle) in London for 38 years. He was part of several controversies with the Baptist Union of Great Britain and later had to leave the denomination. In 1857, he started a charity organization called Spurgeon's which now works globally. He also founded Spurgeon's College, which was named after him posthumously.

Spurgeon was a prolific author of many types of works including sermons, an autobiography, commentaries, books on prayer, devotionals, magazines, poetry, hymns and more. Many sermons were transcribed as he spoke and were translated into many languages during his lifetime. Spurgeon produced powerful sermons of penetrating thought and precise exposition. His oratory skills held throngs of listeners spellbound in the Metropolitan Tabernacle and many Christians have discovered Spurgeon's messages to be among the best in Christian literature.

For an in-depth biographical treatment of C. H. Spurgeon, obtain *From The Usher's Desk to The Tabernacle Pulpit*, also published by Great Christian Books.

THE MISSION OF GREAT CHRISTIAN BOOKS

The ministry of Great Christian Books was established to glorify The Lord Jesus Christ and to be used by Him to expand and edify the kingdom of God while we occupy and anticipate Christ's glorious return. Great Christian Books will seek to accomplish this mission by publishing Gospel literature which is biblically faithful, relevant, and practically applicable to many of the serious spiritual needs of mankind upon the beginning of this new millennium. To do so we will always seek to boldly incorporate the truths of Scripture, especially those which were largely articulated as a body of theology during the Protestant Reformation of the sixteenth century and ensuing years. We gladly join our voice in the proclamations of— Scripture Alone, Faith Alone, Grace Alone, Christ Alone, and God's Glory Alone!

Our ministry seeks the blessing of our God as we seek His face to both confirm and support our labors for Him. Our prayers for this work can be summarized by two verses from the Book of Psalms:

"...let the beauty of the LORD our God be upon us, And establish the work of our hands for us; Yes, establish the work of our hands." —Psalm 90:17

"Not unto us, O LORD, not unto us, but to your name give glory." —Psalm 115:1

Great Christian Books appreciates the financial support of anyone who shares our burden and vision for publishing literature which combines sound Bible doctrine and practical exhortation in an age when too few so-called "Christian" publications do the same. We thank you in advance for any assistance you can give us in our labors to fulfill this important mission. May God bless you.

For a catalog of other great Christian books including additional titles by C. H. Spurgeon contact us in any of the following ways:

www.ingramcontent.com/pod-product-compliance
Lightning Source LLC
LaVergne TN
LVHW041218080426
835508LV00011B/985
* 9 7 8 1 6 1 0 1 0 1 3 0 1 *